THE YALE SHAKESPEARE

Edited by

Wilbur L. Cross   Tucker Brooke

Published under the Direction
of the
Department of English, Yale University,
on the Fund
Given to the Yale University Press in 1917
by the Members of the
Kingsley Trust Association
(Scroll and Key Society of Yale College)
To Commemorate the Seventy-Fifth Anniversary
of the Founding of the Society

THE YALE SHAKESPEARE

Edited by

Wilbur L. Cross   Tucker Brooke

SHAKESPEARE
OF STRATFORD

A HANDBOOK FOR STUDENTS

BY

TUCKER BROOKE

LVX ET VERITAS

NEW HAVEN · YALE UNIVERSITY PRESS
LONDON · GEOFFREY CUMBERLEGE
OXFORD UNIVERSITY PRESS

TABLE OF CONTENTS

The facsimile opposite represents Shakespeare's deposition as witness in the Belott-Mountjoy suit of 1612. See pages 68-69.

The poet's signature at the bottom of the paper is separately reproduced below in the size of the original.

William Shakespeare of Stratford vpon Aven in the Countye of Warwicke gentleman of the age of xlviij yeres or thereaboutes sworne and examined the daye and yere abouesaid deposethe & sayethe

To the first interr: this deponent sayethe he knowethe the partyes plaintiff and deffendant and hathe know them bothe as he now remembrethe for the space of tenne yeres or thereaboutes.

To the second interr: this deponent sayeth he did know the complainant when he was servant with the deffendant, and that duringe the tyme of his the complainantes service with the said deffendant he the said complainant to this deponentes knowledge did well and honestly behaue himselfe, but to this deponentes remembrance he hath not heard the deffendant confesse that he had gott any great profitt and comodytye by the service of the said complainant, but this deponent saithe he verely thinkethe that the said complainant was a very good and industrious servant in the said service. And more he canott depose to the said interr:

To the third interr: this deponent sayethe that it did evydentlye appeare that the said deffendant did all the tyme of the said complainantes service with him beare and shew great good will and affeccion towardes the said complainant, and that he hath hard the deffendant and his wyefe diuerse and sundry tymes saye and reporte that the said complainant was a very honest fellow: And this deponent sayethe that the said deffendant did make a mocion vnto the complainant of marriadge with the said Mary in the bill mencioned beinge the said deffendantes sole chyld and daughter, and willinglye offered to performe the same yf the said complainant shold seeme to be content and well like thereof: And further this deponent sayethe that the said deffendantes wyeffe did sollicitt and entreat this deponent to moue and perswade the said complainant to effect the said marriadge, and accordingly this deponent did moue and perswade the complainant thervnto: And more to this interrogatory he cannott depose

To the ffourth interr: this deponent sayth that the defendant promissed to geue the said complainant a porcion in marriadge with Marye his daughter, but what certayne porcion he rememberethe not, nor when to be payed, nor knoweth that the defendant promissed the plaintiff twoe hundered poundes with his daughter Marye at the tyme of his decease. But sayth that the plaintiff was dwellinge with the defendant in his house, and they had amongeste them selues manye conferences about there marriadge which was consumated and solempnized. And more he cann

To the vth interr: this deponent sayth he can saye noth touchinge any parte or poynte of the same interr: for he knoweth not what implementes and necessaries of houshold stuffe the defendant gaue the plaintiff in marriadge with his daughter Marye.

Willm Shakp

THE BIOGRAPHICAL FACTS

[English documents are given in modern spelling, except as regards proper names, which remain as in the originals. Latin documents are usually not normalized, but are translated in footnotes.]

I. SHAKESPEARE'S BIRTH (1564).

Baptismal Register, Stratford-on-Avon.

1564 April 26 Gulielmus filius Johannes Shakspere.

NOTE ONE. The Date of Shakespeare's Birth is not precisely known, but it probably preceded his baptism on April 26 by only a few days. The tradition is that he was born on St. George's Day, April 23, which was the day also on which he died. The inscription on his monument stating that he was 'Ætatis 53' at his decease would indicate that he had at least completed his fifty-second year on April 23, 1616.

NOTE TWO. Shakespeare's Parents and Ancestry.

The poet's paternal grandfather was probably Richard Shakespeare (d. 1561), a farmer of Snitterfield, four miles northeast of Stratford. The poet's father, John Shakespeare, was living in Henley Street, Stratford, in 1552. In 1561 he was elected one of the two chamberlains of the borough; in 1565 he became an alderman; and in 1568 high bailiff, or mayor, of the town. He was buried, September 8, 1601.

John Shakespeare married (presumably in 1557) Mary Arden, youngest daughter of Robert Arden, a wealthy landowner of Wilmecote, a couple of miles north of Stratford. Robert Arden, who had died in 1556, was the son of Thomas Arden (the poet's maternal great-grandfather), who was living at Wilmecote in 1501 and who probably belonged to the aristocratic family of the Ardens of Park Hall.[1] Mary Shakespeare, the poet's mother, was buried at Stratford, September 9, 1608.

NOTE THREE. Shakespeare's Brothers and Sisters.

The poet was the third child and first son of John and Mary Shakespeare. The other children, with their dates of baptism were:

> Joan (Sept. 15, 1558),
> Margaret (Dec. 2, 1562),
> Gilbert (Oct. 13, 1566),
> Joan (Apr. 15, 1569),
> Anne (Sept. 28, 1571),
> Richard (Mar. 11, 1574),
> Edmund (May 3, 1580).

The first two daughters died in infancy, and Anne (buried Apr. 4, 1579) at the age of seven. The poet's three brothers all died before him, probably without children, though Gilbert may possibly have had a son.[2] Edmund became an actor and was buried in St. Saviour's Church, Southwark, Dec. 31, 1607. Joan—the second sister so named—married William Hart and has descendants still alive.

II. SHAKESPEARE'S MARRIAGE (1582).

(A) Record of issue of marriage license, Episcopal Register, Diocese of Worcester, November 27, 1582:

1 See Mrs. C. C. Stopes, *Shakespeare's Family*, p. 49; *Shakespeare's Environment*, pp. 47 ff.
2 Against this possibility cf. *Shakespeare's Environment*, pp. 332 ff.

Anno Domini 1582 . . . Novembris . . . 27 die eiusdem mensis. Item eodem die supradicto emanavit Licentia inter Wm Shaxpere et Annam Whateley de Temple Grafton.[1]

(B) Marriage Bond from Worcester Episcopal Registry, November 28, 1582:

Noverint universi per praesentes nos Fulconem Sandells de Stratford in comitatu Warwici agricolam et Johannem Rychardson ibidem agricolam, teneri et firmiter obligari Ricardo Cosin generoso et Roberto Warmstry notario publico in quadraginta libris bonae et legalis monetae Angliae solvend. eisdem Ricardo et Roberto haered. execut. et assignat. suis ad quam quidem solucionem bene et fideliter faciend. obligamus nos et utrumque nostrum per se pro toto et in solid. haered. executor. et administrator. nostros firmiter per praesentes sigillis nostris sigillat. Dat. 28 die Novem. Anno regni dominae nostrae Eliz. Dei gratia Angliae Franc. et Hiberniae Reginae fidei defensor &c. 25°.[2]

The condition of this obligation is such that if hereafter there shall not appear any lawful let or impediment by reason of any precontract, consanguinity, affinity or by any other lawful means whatsoever, but that Willm Shagspere on the one party and Anne Hathwey of Stratford in the diocese of Worcester,

1 'Likewise on the same day aforesaid there went out a license [for marriage] between Wm. Shaxpere and Anne Whateley of Temple Grafton.' (Latin abbreviations have been expanded.)

2 'Let all know by these presents that we, Fulke Sandells of Stratford in the county of Warwick yeoman and John Richardson of the same place yeoman, are held and firmly bound to Richard Cosin gentleman and Robert Warmstry notary public in the sum of forty pounds of good and legal English money to be paid to the same Richard and Robert, their heirs, executors, and assigns, for the good and faithful performance of which payment we firmly bind ourselves and each of us individually for the whole, our heirs, executors, and administrators, by this paper sealed with our seals. Given the 28th day of November in the twenty-fifth year of the reign of our lady Elizabeth, by the grace of God Queen of England, France, and Ireland, defender of the faith, etc.'

*maiden, may lawfully solemnize matrimony together,
and in the same afterwards remain and continue like
man and wife according unto the laws in that behalf
provided; and moreover if there be not at this present
time any action, suit, quarrel, or demand moved or de-
pending before any judge ecclesiastical or temporal
for and concerning any such lawful let or impediment;
and moreover if the said Willm do not proceed to
solemnization of marriage with the said Anne Hathwey
without the consent of her friends; and also if the said
Willm do upon his own proper costs and expenses
defend and save harmless the right reverend Father
in God, Lord John Bishop of Worcester and his officers
for licensing them the said Willm and Anne to be married together with once asking of the bans of matrimony between them and for all other causes which may
ensue by reason or occasion thereof: that then the
said obligation to be void and of none effect or else
to stand and abide in full force and virtue.*

NOTE ONE.   Anne Whateley of Temple Grafton.

It is probable, but not certain, that the Anne Whateley mentioned in document A as the intended wife of
Wm. Shaxpere is the same as the Anne Hathwey of
document B, and that both records therefore refer to
the poet.   Sir Sidney Lee (*Life of Shakespeare*, 1922,
pp. 30 f.) argues against the identity of the two; Mrs.
Stopes (*Shakespeare's Family*, p. 63), J. W. Gray
(*Shakespeare's Marriage*, p. 23), and Professor J. Q.
Adams (*Life of Shakespeare*, p. 76), cite good reasons
for accepting it.   Whateley was a name of not infre-
quent occurrence in the Worcester neighborhood and
might be misread or otherwise inadvertently substituted
by the clerk for Hathwey.   Temple Grafton is a village

five miles from Stratford and may have been the place selected for the wedding—presumably because the Stratford rector declined to perform it or because the couple desired to avoid publicity. The Temple Grafton marriage register for the period is lost, and no record of the actual marriage of Shakespeare and Anne Hathway has been found elsewhere.

NOTE TWO. Anne Hathway.

Anne Hathway, or Hathaway, was probably the eldest daughter, and one of the seven children, of Richard Hathway of Shottery in the parish of Old Stratford, whose will was dated Sept. 1, 1581, and proved July 9, 1582. She was buried as 'Mrs. Shakspeare' at Stratford, August 8, 1623, having died at New Place two days before, and was interred beside her husband in the chancel of the church with the following inscription: 'Here lieth interred the body of Anne, wife of Mr. William Shakespeare, who departed this life the 6th day of August, 1623, being of the age of 67 years.' The note of her age indicates that she was seven or eight years older than the poet. There exists no other evidence for the date of her birth.

NOTE THREE. The Marriage Bond (Document B).

The two signers of the bond were friends of the Hathway family, evidently acting in the interests of Anne. Richard Hathway's will names Fulke Sandells as one of his two 'trusty friends and neighbors' whom he appoints as supervisors of the testament; and John Richardson appears as one of the witnesses to it. The absence of any reference to Shakespeare's family has been cited as a striking irregularity in the document, particularly as the poet was a minor. On the other hand it is argued that John Shakespeare's embarrassed financial condition in 1582 would have rendered him unacceptable as surety for so large a bond as forty pounds, and that the license would not have been issued at all unless the Bishop's representatives had received satisfactory assurance that he would not make serious complaint about the marriage.

The purpose of the bond and Bishop's license was to save time. Normal procedure in the case of marriages was by thrice reading the bans on successive weeks; but December 1, 1582, began a prohibited period in the church year, the effect of which would have been to postpone for about two months the performance of the ceremony by the ordinary method.

III. BIRTH OF SHAKESPEARE'S DAUGHTER, SUSANNA (1583).

Baptismal Register, Stratford-on-Avon.

1583 May 26 Susanna, daughter to William Shakspere.

NOTE. Susanna Shakespeare married John Hall of Stratford, an eminent physician, June 5, 1607, and died July 11, 1649. She had one daughter, Elizabeth Hall (baptized February 21, 1608), who married successively Thomas Nash of Welcombe near Stratford (April 22, 1626) and John Bernard, later Sir John Bernard, of Northamptonshire (June 5, 1649). She died without issue, February 17, 1670, being the poet's last living descendant.

IV. BIRTH OF SHAKESPEARE'S TWIN CHILDREN (1585).

Baptismal Register, Stratford.

1584 [i.e. 1585] *February 2 Hamnet and Judeth, son and daughter to William Shakspere.*

NOTE. The twin children were presumably named after Hamnet Sadler, a baker of Stratford, and his wife Judith. Fripp (*Richard Quyny,* p. 108) notes that Hamnet and Hamlet are interchangeable spellings in the Stratford town records.[1]

Hamnet Shakespeare was buried August 11, 1596, having lived eleven and a half years. (See no. XII.) Judith married Thomas Quyny of Stratford (Feb. 10, 1616) and was buried there February 9, 1662, aged seventy-seven. She had three sons, all of whom died long before her and unmarried. The eldest, Shakespeare Quyny (baptized November 23, 1616), lived less than six months.

V. MENTION OF SHAKESPEARE AS HEIR OF JOHN AND MARY SHAKESPEARE IN SUIT OVER THE ESTATE OF ASBIES (1589).

From Coram Rege Roll, Public Record Office, London.

In 1579 John and Mary Shakespeare alienated to Edmund Lambert, brother-in-law of Mary, for forty pounds, the estate of Asbies, three miles from Stratford, an inheritance from Mary's father, Robert Arden. There appears to have been an informal agreement for recovery of the estate on repayment of the sum; but Edmund and after him his son, John Lambert, refused to acknowledge this. In Michaelmas term (autumn), 1589, John Shakespeare brought suit against John Lambert, asserting that on Edmund Lambert's death in 1587, John Lambert contracted to pay twenty pounds on condition that the Shakespeares should not bring suit against him and should confirm him in the possession of the estate. The por-

1 See p. 84, fifth line from bottom.

tion of the document mentioning William Shakespeare is as follows:

Et quod dictus Johannes Shackespere et Maria uxor ejus, simul cum Willielmo Shackespere filio suo, cum inde requisiti essent, assurarent mesuagium predictum et cetera premissa, cum pertinentiis, prefato Johanni Lamberte, et deliberarent omnia scripta et evidencias premissa predicta concernentia; predictus Johannes Lamberte vicesimo sexto die Septembris anno regni dicte domine regine vicesimo nono, apud Stratford-super-Avon in comitatu predicto, in consideracione inde super se assumpsit et prefato Johanni Shackespere, adtunc et ibidem fideliter promisit quod ipse, idem Johannes Lambert, viginti libras legalis monete Anglie prefato Johanni Shackespere . . . bene et fideliter solvere et contentare vellet; et predictus Johannes Shackespere in facto dicit quod ipse hucusque non im-placitavit dictum Johannem Lambert pro premissis, nec aliqua inde parcella, et insuper quod ipse, idem Johannes Shackespere et Maria uxor ejus, simul cum Willielmo Shackespere filio suo semper hactenus parati fuerunt tam ad assurandum premissa predicta quam ad deliberandum eidem Johanni Lamberte omnia scripta et evidencias eadem premissa concernentia; predictus tamen Johannes Lamberte, promissionem et assumpcionem suas predictas minime curans, sed machinans et fraudulenter intendens ipsum Johannem Shackespere de predictis viginti libris callide et sub-dole decipere et defraudare, easdem viginti libras prefato Johanni Shackespere juxta promissionem et assumpcionem suas hucusque non solvit. . . . [1]

[1] 'And that the said John Shakespeare and Mary his wife, together with William Shakespeare their son, when they should be asked to do so, would confirm the aforesaid messuage and other premises with their appurtenances to the said John Lambert, and would deliver all writings and evidences concerning the aforesaid

NOTE. Nothing seems to have been effected by this suit, in which the poet was only indirectly concerned. Eight years later (Nov. 24, 1597) a chancery suit against Lambert was instituted in the name of John and Mary Shakespeare, but doubtless at the expense of the poet, who however is not mentioned. The case dragged on for several years without profit to the Shakespeares. The documents are given by Halliwell-Phillipps, *Outlines,* 7th ed., ii. 14 ff.

VI. GREENE'S INDICTMENT OF SHAKESPEARE AS 'JOHANNES FAC TOTUM' OF THE THEATRE (1592).

Epilogue to Robert Greene's *Groatsworth of Wit, bought with a Million of Repentance* (August-September, 1592).

To those gentlemen, his quondam acquaintance, that spend their wits in making plays, R. G. wisheth a better exercise, and wisdom to prevent his extremities. . . .

Base minded men all three of you, if by my misery you be not warned: for unto none of you (like me) sought those burs to cleave, those puppets (I mean) that spake from our mouths, those antics garnished in our colors. Is it not strange that I, to whom they all

premises. The aforesaid John Lambert, on the twenty-sixth day of September in the twenty-ninth year of the reign of our said lady the Queen (1587), at Stratford-on-Avon in the aforesaid county, in consideration of this took upon himself and then and there faithfully promised the said John Shakespeare that he, the same John Lambert, would well and faithfully pay and satisfy to the said John Shakespeare twenty pounds of legal money of England; and the said J. S. says in fact that he has not hitherto sued the said J. L. for the premises nor any part of them, and moreover that he the said J. S. and Mary his wife, together with William Shakespeare their son, have always been ready both to confirm [J. L.'s possession of] the aforesaid premises and to deliver to the same J. L. all writings and evidences concerning the said premises. Nevertheless the said J. L., very little regarding his promise and undertaking aforesaid, but scheming and fraudulently intending to deceive and defraud J. S. of the said twenty pounds, has not hitherto paid the twenty pounds to the said J. S. according to his promise and undertaking.'

have been beholding: is it not like that you, to whom they all have been beholding, shall (were ye in that case as I am now) be both at once of them forsaken? Yes, trust them not: for there is an upstart crow, beautified with our feathers, that with his Tiger's heart wrapt in a player's hide *supposes he is as well able to bombast out a blank verse as the best of you; and being an absolute* Johannes fac totum, *is in his own conceit the only Shake-scene in a country. O that I might intreat your rare wits to be employed in more profitable courses, and let those apes imitate your past excellence, and never more acquaint them with your admired inventions.*

NOTE. Greene's *Groatsworth of Wit* was written during the last illness of the author, who died September 3, 1592. The title-page of the edition of that year states that the book was 'written before his death and published at his dying request.' The actor-playwright attacked as 'an upstart crow,' 'an absolute *Johannes fac totum,*' and 'the only Shake-scene' is undoubtedly Shakespeare. The three acquaintances of Greene whom he exhorts to give up play-writing are pretty evidently Marlowe, Peele, and Nashe. The last two are addressed in friendly and flattering terms, but the address to Marlowe (who is called 'famous gracer of tragedians,' atheist, and student of 'pestilent Machiavellian policy') has a bitter tone.

VII. CHETTLE'S APOLOGY TO SHAKE-SPEARE (1592).

Preface to Henry Chettle's *Kind-Heart's Dream,* December, 1592.

About three months since died M. Robert Greene,

leaving many papers in sundry booksellers' hands, among other his Groatsworth of Wit, in which a letter written to divers play-makers is offensively by one or two of them taken, and because on the dead they cannot be avenged, they wilfully forge in their conceits a living author. . . . With neither of them that take offence was I acquainted, and with one of them I care not if I never be. The other, whom at that time I did not so much spare as since I wish I had, for that, as I have moderated the heat of living writers and might have used my own discretion (especially in such a case, the author being dead), that I did not I am as sorry as if the original fault had been my fault, because myself have seen his demeanor no less civil than he excellent in the quality he professes. Besides, divers of worship have reported his uprightness of dealing, which argues his honesty, and his facetious grace in writing that approves his art.

NOTE. It appears that Marlowe and Shakespeare, personally or through their friends, had resented the allusions in Greene's *Groatsworth*, posthumously published under the editorship of Chettle. The playmaker with whom Chettle does not wish to be acquainted is almost certainly Marlowe; and the other, whose 'uprightness of dealing' and 'facetious grace in writing' Chettle praises, is undoubtedly Shakespeare.

VIII. SHAKESPEARE'S FORMAL DEBUT AS A POET (1593).

Dedication of *Venus and Adonis* to the Earl of Southampton.

To the Right Honorable Henry Wriothesley, Earl of Southampton, and Baron of Titchfield.

Right Honorable: I know not how I shall offend in dedicating my unpolished lines to your Lordship, nor how the world will censure me for choosing so strong a prop to support so weak a burthen; only if your Honor seem but pleased, I account myself highly praised, and vow to take advantage of all idle hours till I have honored you with some graver labor. But if the first heir of my invention prove deformed, I shall be sorry it had so noble a godfather, and never after ear [plough] so barren a land for fear it yield me still so bad a harvest. I leave it to your honorable survey, and your Honor to your heart's content, which I wish may always answer your own wish and the world's hopeful expectation.

> *Your Honor's in all duty,*
> ### WILLIAM SHAKESPEARE.

NOTE. *Venus and Adonis* was entered for publication, April 18, 1593, by Richard Field, son of a tanner of Stratford. Field, who was three years older than Shakespeare, had left Stratford in 1579 and become a member of the Stationers' Company in London.

IX. SHAKESPEARE'S ACKNOWLEDGMENT OF SOUTHAMPTON'S PATRONAGE (1594).

Dedication of *Lucrece.*

To the Right Honorable Henry Wriothesley, Earl of Southampton, and Baron of Titchfield.

The love I dedicate to your Lordship is without end; whereof this pamphlet without beginning is but a superfluous moiety. The warrant I have of your honorable disposition, not the worth of my untutored lines, makes it assured of acceptance. What I have done is yours, what I have to do is yours, being part

*in all I have, devoted yours. Were my worth greater,
my duty would show greater; meantime, as it is, it is
bound to your Lordship, to whom I wish long life
still lengthened with all happiness.*

      Your Lordship's in all duty,
        WILLIAM SHAKESPEARE.

NOTE. *Lucrece* was licensed for printing, May 9,
1594. Southampton's generous patronage of the poet
is the subject of an anecdote in Rowe's *Life of Shakespeare* (1709) to the effect that the Earl on one occasion presented Shakespeare with a thousand pounds
to enable him to carry through a purchase he had in
mind.

X. THE EARLIEST TRIBUTE TO SHAKE-SPEARE BY NAME AS A POET (1594).

Anonymous verses prefixed to *Willobie His Avisa*
(1594).

*Though Collatine have dearly bought
  To high renown a lasting life,
And found that [what] most in vain have sought,
  To have a fair and constant wife;
    Yet Tarquin plucked his glistering grape,
    And Shake-speare paints poor Lucrece' rape.*

NOTE. This illustrates the immediate popularity of
Shakespeare's *Lucrece*. The curious topical work in
mingled prose and verse which this commendatory
poem introduces comprises a dialogue between H. W.
(Henry Willobie) and one W. S. It has been dubiously
supposed to allude to Shakespeare as an authority on
love. The book was entered for publication, September 3, 1594.

XI. FIRST RECORD OF SHAKESPEARE AS A LEADING MEMBER OF THE LORD CHAMBERLAIN'S COMPANY OF PLAYERS (1594/5).

Manuscript Accounts of the Treasurer of the Royal Chamber in Public Record Office.

1594 [i.e. 1595] *March 15 To William Kempe, William Shakespeare, and Richard Burbage, servants to the Lord Chamberlain, upon the Council's warrant dated at Whitehall xv die Marcij 1594 for two several comedies or interludes showed by them before her Majesty in Christmas time last past, viz.; upon St. Stephen's day and Innocents' day, xiij li. vj s. viij d., and by way of her Majesty's reward vj li. xiij s. iiij d.: in all, xx li.*

NOTE. This shows that Shakespeare had performed in plays before Queen Elizabeth on Dec. 26 and Dec. 28, 1594, the court being then at Greenwich Palace. For each play the company, for which Shakespeare was one of the three payees, received ten pounds, two-thirds of that amount being reckoned the proper price of the performance and one-third the Queen's additional gratuity. (See Mrs. Stopes, 'The Earliest Official Record of Shakespeare's Name,' in *Shakespeare's Industry*, pp. 218 ff., where it is conjectured that one of the comedies presented was *The Comedy of Errors.*)

There is no earlier documentary evidence regarding the particular company with which Shakespeare was connected. It has been commonly assumed that he joined the predecessors of the Chamberlain's company as soon as he reached London or even earlier. Recent investigators, however, have argued from cir-

cumstantial evidence that his first connection was
rather with Lord Pembroke's players. (See J. Q.
Adams, *Life of Shakespeare*, 1923, pp. 130 ff., and
R. Crompton Rhodes, *Shakespeare's First Folio*, 1923,
pp. 84 ff.)

XII. BURIAL OF SHAKESPEARE'S SON (1596).

Stratford Burial Register.

1596   August 11   Hamnet filius William Shakspere.

XIII. DRAFT OF GRANT OF ARMS TO SHAKE-SPEARE'S FATHER (1596).

Rough draft, preserved in Heralds' College, London,
of arms devised for John Shakespeare by William
Dethick, Oct. 20, 1596.

NON SANZ DROICT   *Shakespere, 1596.*

*To all and singular, noble and gentlemen, of what
estate or degree bearing arms, to whom these presents
shall come, William Dethick, alias Garter, principal
king of arms, sendeth greetings. Know ye that whereas
by the authority and ancient privilege and custom per-
taining to my said office of principal king of arms from
the Queen's most excellent majesty and her highness'
most noble and victorious progenitors I am to take
general notice and record, and to make public demon-
stration and testimony, for all causes of arms and
matters of gentry throughout all her Majesty's kingdoms and dominions, principalities, isles, and provinces
to the end that as some by their ancient names, families,
kindreds, and descents have and enjoy sundry en-
signs and [coats] of arms, so other for their valiant
facts, magnanimity, virtue, dignities, and deserts
may have such marks and tokens of honor and worthi-
ness whereby their name and good fame shall be [the*

*better known] and divulged and their children and
posterity in all virtue to the service of their prince and
country [encouraged]. Being therefore solicited and
[by] credible report informed that John Shakespeare
of Stratford-upon-Avon in the county of Warwick,
whose parents and late antecessors were for their
valiant and faithful service advanced and rewarded by
the most prudent prince King Henry the Seventh of
famous memory, sithence which time they have continued in those parts in good reputation and credit, and
that the said John having married Mary, daughter
and one of the heirs of Robert Arden of Wilmcote in
the said county, Esq. In consideration whereof and for
encouragement of his posterity, to whom these achievements may [?] descend by the ancient custom and
laws of arms, I have therefore assigned, granted, and
by these presents confirmed this shield or coat of arms;
viz., Gold on a bend sable a spear of the first, the point
steeled, proper; and for his crest or cognizance a falcon, his wings displayed, argent, standing on a wreath
of his colors, supporting a spear—gold—steeled as
aforesaid, set upon a helmet with mantels and tassels
as hath been accustomed and more plainly appeareth
depicted on this margent. Signifying hereby that it
shall be lawful for the said John Shakespeare, Gent.,
and for his children, issue, and posterity at all times
convenient to make show of and to bear blazoned the
same achievement on their shield or coat of arms,
escutcheons, crest, cognizance or seals, rings, signets,
pennons, guidons, edifices [?], utensils, liveries, tombs,
or monuments, or otherwise, at all times in all lawful
warlike facts or civil use and exercises, according to
the laws of arms without let or interruption of any
other person or persons. In witness whereof I have*

hereunto subscribed my name and fastened the seal of my office endorsed with the signet of my arms. At the Office of Arms, London, the xx. day of October, the xxxix. [i.e. 38th] year of the reign of our Sovereign Lady Elizabeth, by the grace of God Queen of England, France and Ireland, defender of the faith, etc. 1596.

NOTE. The document quoted above is a very rough draft, with many interlineations. Dethick made a copy of it, introducing some unimportant verbal changes, which is also in the Heralds' Office, but the fairer copy is badly torn in two places. Bracketed words in the transcript above are supplied from the second copy. Both documents give on the margin a pen and ink sketch of the arms assigned to Shakespeare. The second draft has the following notes added at the bottom:

This John hath a pattern thereof under Clarenc. Cooke's hand in paper xx. years past. A justice of peace, and was bailiff, officer, and chief of the town of Stratford-upon-Avon xv or xvi years past. That he hath lands and tenements of good wealth and substance, 500 li. That he mar—(remainder missing).

Good facsimiles of both papers are provided in *Miscellanea Genealogica et Heraldica*, edited by J. J. Howard, Second Series, vol. i, p. 109 (1886).

It is reasonably conjectured that the motive for John Shakespeare's effort thus to establish his social position came from the poet, and that it reflects the latter's ambition and worldly prosperity. Other wealthy actors—e.g. Augustine Phillips and Thomas Pope of Shakespeare's company—assumed arms to which they appear to have had no hereditary right.

A contemporary herald, Ralph Brooke, mentions Shakespeare as one of twenty-three persons charged with obtaining coats of arms to which they were not entitled. (For an answer to this accusation see Mrs. Stopes, *Shakespeare's Family,* pp. 22 f.) The arms here granted are displayed on the monument above Shakespeare's grave and on the tombstone of his daughter Susanna. For a later document granting heraldic honors to Shakespeare see no. XXVI.

XIV. SHAKESPEARE ASSESSED FOR TAXES AS A RESIDENT OF ST. HELEN'S PARISH, BISHOPSGATE (1596-1598).

The following documents are in the Public Record Office, London.

(A) Report of collectors of the subsidy, November 15, 1597.

The petty collectors of the said second payment of the said last subsidy within the ward of Bishopsgate, London . . . did say and affirm that the persons hereunder named are all either dead, departed, and gone out of the said ward, or their goods so eloigned or conveyed out of the same or in such a private or covert manner kept, whereby the several sums of money on them severally taxed and assessed towards the said second payment of the said last subsidy neither might nor could by any means by them the said petty collectors, or either of them, be levied of them, or any of them, to her Majesty's use.

Among the defaulters in *St. Ellen's parish* is listed *William Shackspere V li.—v s.*[1]

1 The meaning of this is that Shakespeare was assessed as owning personal property to the value of five pounds in the parish and was taxed at the rate of one shilling in the pound. He had evidently removed from the parish before the collectors called.

(B) Assessment paper, October 1, 1598.

This indenture, made the first day of October, in the fortieth year of the reign of our Sovereign Lady, Elizabeth . . . Witnesseth that the said Ferdinando Clutterbooke and Thomas Symons so named, deputed, appointed, and chosen to be petty collectors in the said ward [i.e. Bishopsgate], *and authorized thereunto by these presents, shall receive, levy, collect, and gather of all and every the several persons hereafter named to the Queen's Majesty's use all such several sams of money as in this present extract been taxed and assessed upon them and every of them, for their several values and substances, rated, specified, and contained as hereafter followeth; that is to say, of*

.   .   .   .

St. Helen's Parish.

.   .   .   .

Affid. William Shakespeare, V li.—xiii[s] *iv*[d].[1]

(C) Residuum, or back-tax, account for London, 1598.

William Shakspeare in the parish of St. Helen's in Bishopsgate Ward owes 13s. 4d. of the subsidy; and he answers in the following roll[2] *in Residuum Sussex.*

(D) Residuum account for Sussex (which included also the Bankside district in Surrey), 1599.

William Shakspeare in the parish of St. Helen, 13s. 4d. of the whole subsidy aforesaid granted in the said

---

1 The meaning of 'Affid.' is uncertain. Hales interprets it as signifying that Shakespeare protested the tax. It is affixed to the names of six other residents of St. Helen's and to the names of thirteen persons listed as 'strangers' in the parish. The tax in this case was at the rate of two shillings and eightpence in the pound.
2 This means that in the tax lists of the following year he will be found in the Residuum for Sussex, not London.

39th year. Which is required upon the same roll there.

This is annotated in the margin, *'Episcopo Wintonensi,'* meaning that the person referred to was under the jurisdiction of the Bishop of Winchester, who controlled the Bankside district.

NOTE. The second of these documents was first pointed out by Joseph Hunter, *Illustrations of Shakespeare,* 1845, 76-79; the others by J. W. Hales, *Athenaeum,* March 26, 1904. They indicate that Shakespeare had resided, probably for a number of years, in St. Helen's parish, which was near the Shoreditch theatres ('Theatre' and 'Curtain'), but that he had removed before 1597 and by 1599 had been traced by the inefficient tax collectors to the Bishop of Winchester's liberty (i.e. the Bankside in Southwark). He seems then to have discharged the debt, as his name does not appear in the list of delinquents for the next year.

Confirmation of Shakespeare's removal to Southwark is found in an uncorroborated note by Malone: 'From a paper now before me, which formerly belonged to Edward Alleyn, the player, our poet appears to have lived in Southwark, near the Bear Garden, in 1596.'

XV. SHAKESPEARE PURCHASES 'NEW PLACE' IN STRATFORD (1597).

'Foot of fine' (essential part) of deed transferring New Place from William Underhill to William Shakespeare, Easter Term (May 4), 1597. In Public Record Office.

Inter Willm Shakespeare, querentem, et Willm

*Underhill, generosum, deforciantem, de uno mesuagio,
duobus horreis, et duobus gardinis cum pertinenciis in
Stratford super Avon, unde placitum convencionis
summonitum fuit inter eos in eadem curia, Scilicet quod
predictus Wills. Underhill recognovit predicta tenementa cum pertinenciis esse jus ipsius Willi. Shakespeare ut illa que idem Wills. habet de dono predicti
Willi. Underhill, et illa remisit et quietumclamavit de
se et heredibus suis predicto Willo. Shakespeare et
heredibus suis imperpetuum; et preterea idem Wills.
Underhill concessit pro se et heredibus suis quod ipsi
warantizabunt predicto Willo. Shakespeare et heredibus suis predicta tenementa cum pertinenciis imperpetuum; et pro hac recognicione, remissione, quieta
clamancia, warancia, fine, et concordia idem Wills
Shakespeare dedit predicto Willo. Underhill sexaginta
libras sterlingorum. In cuius rei testimonium . . .*

iiij° die Maii anno regni supradicto.[1]

NOTE. New Place, the second largest house in Stratford, was built over a century before Shakespeare
acquired it by a member of the important Clopton
family. It stood at the corner of Chapel Street and
Chapel Lane, north of the Guild Chapel. In 1563 the
house passed from the possession of William Clopton

1 'Between William Shakespeare, complainant, and William Underhill, deforciant [wrongful occupier, supposed by the legal fiction on
which the 'fine' method of transfer was based to be keeping the complainant out of his rightful property], concerning one dwelling house,
two barns, and two gardens with their appurtenances in Stratford-on-
Avon, in regard to which a plea of agreement was broached in the
same court: Namely, that the said William Underhill acknowledged
the said tenements with their appurtenances to be the right of W.
Shakespeare as being those which the same William [Shakespeare]
has by gift of the said W. U., and remitted and waived claim to
them from himself and his heirs to the said W. S. and his heirs
forever; and moreover the same W. U. has agreed for himself and
his heirs that they will assure the said tenements with their appurtenances to the said W. S. and his heirs forever; and for this
acknowledgment, remission, quit-claim, waranty, fine, and agreement
the same W.S. has given the foresaid W. U. sixty pounds ster-
ling. . . .'

to that of a wealthy, though apparently unscrupulous, capitalist, William Bott, who sold it in 1567 to William Underhill, father of the William who appears as vendor in the sale to Shakespeare. Shakespeare's family entered into occupation of the house very shortly after he had purchased it, but a further transaction with a member of the Underhill family became necessary in 1602 to assure the poet's title (see document XXXV). New Place remained Shakespeare's home till his death, and his will makes elaborate provision for its transfer to his heirs, who continued to own it till the death in 1670 of Lady Bernard, his granddaughter and last lineal descendant. In accordance with Lady Bernard's will the house was sold, and ultimately passed back to the Clopton family, one of whom in 1702 erected a new house on the site of the Shakespearean mansion. (See Halliwell-Phillipps, *Outlines of the Life of Shakespeare,* seventh ed., 1887, ii. 101-135, for a full account of the history of New Place.)

XVI. SHAKESPEARE INTERESTED IN PURCHASES OF LAND AT SHOTTERY (1598).

Letter of Abraham Sturley of Stratford to Richard Quyny, temporarily in London, January 24, 1598. (Stratford Corporation Records.)

Most loving and beloved in the Lord, in plain English we remember you in the Lord and ourselves unto you. I would write nothing unto you now but 'Come home!' I pray God send you comfortably home. This is one special remembrance from your father's[1] motion: It seemeth by him that our countryman, Mr. Shaksper,

---

1 Richard Quyny's father, Adrian Quyny, a neighbor and close associate of John Shakespeare from 1552. Like the poet's father he had served as Bailiff of the town, and in 1572 was joined with John Shakespeare in a mission to London on corporation business.

is willing to disburse some money upon some odd yardland[1] or other at Shottery or near about us. He thinketh it a very fit pattern to move him to deal in the matter of our tithes. By the instructions you can give him thereof, and by the friends he can make therefor, we think it a fair mark for him to shoot at, and not unpossible to hit. It obtained would advance him indeed, and would do us much good. Hoc movere et, quantum in te est, permovere ne negligas: hoc enim et sibi et nobis maximi erit momenti. Hic labor, hic opus esset eximie et gloriae et laudis sibi.[2]

You shall understand, brother, that our neighbors are grown, with the wants they feel through the dearness of corn, which here is beyond all other countries[3] that I can hear of dear and over-dear, malcontent. They have assembled together in a great number, and travelled to Sir Thomas Lucy on Friday last to complain of our maltsters; on Sunday to Sir Fulke Greville and Sir John Conway. I should have said on Wednesday to Sir Edward Greville first. There is a meeting here expected to-morrow. The Lord knoweth to what end it will sort.[4]

NOTE. Richard Quyny, to whom this letter is addressed, is the writer of the only extant letter addressed to Shakespeare (see document XXI). His life has been written by E. I. Fripp: *Master Richard Quyny, Bailiff of Stratford-upon-Avon and Friend of William Shakespeare* (1924). Abraham Sturley had been a student at Queens' College, Cambridge, had

---

1 A yardland was a section of about thirty acres.

2 'Do not fail to urge this and, as far as you can, to urge it thoroughly; for this will be of the greatest consequence both to him and to us. This would be a labor, this a work, of surpassing honor and credit to him [i.e. Shakespeare].'

3 I.e. districts, counties.

4 In connection with this paragraph of Sturley's letter see the next document.

been elected Bailiff of Stratford in 1596. He was a legal and business agent, doing business for Sir Thomas Lucy among others.

XVII. SHAKESPEARE LISTED AMONG THE CHIEF HOLDERS OF CORN AND MALT IN STRATFORD (1598).

Stratford Corporation Records.

Stratford Borough, Warwick. The note of corn and malt taken the iiijth of February, 1597 [i.e. 1598], *in the xlth year of the reign of our most gracious sovereign lady, Queen Elizabeth, &c. Chapel Street Ward. . . . Wm. Shackespere, x quarters.*

NOTE. The occasion of this inventory was a shortage of grain and its object was to prevent hoarding. Chapel Street Ward is the one in which New Place was situated. Ten quarters is eighty bushels; only two residents of the ward are credited with a larger amount than Shakespeare. It is noted that Sir Thomas Lucy had sixteen quarters in the custody of Richard Dixon and twelve and a half quarters in that of Abraham Sturley.

XVIII. SHAKESPEARE'S NAME BEGINS TO APPEAR ON THE TITLE-PAGES OF HIS PLAYS (1598).

(A) *Richard II* (second and third editions).[1]

The Tragedy of King Richard the Second. As it hath been publicly acted by the Right Honourable the Lord Chamberlain his Servants. By William Shake-speare. . . . 1598.

1 Two editions of the play, only recently distinguished, were printed in 1598, both with Shakespeare's name on the title-page.

NOTE. Quyny was in London for eighteen weeks, from October, 1598, till February, 1599, in a laborious and ultimately successful endeavor to secure government relief from certain taxes recently imposed upon Stratford. His correspondence suggests that he secured without delay the loan of thirty pounds from Shakespeare. Cf. Fripp, *Master Richard Quyny*, p. 139.

XXII. ALLUSIONS TO SHAKESPEARE'S LOAN TO QUYNY (1598).

(A) Extract from undated letter (ca. November 1, 1598) from Adrian Quyny of Stratford to his son Richard in London. (Corporation Records, Stratford.)

If you bargain with Wm. Sha. . or receive money there, bring your money home that you may; and see how knit stockings be sold. There is great buying of them at Evesham. Edward Wheat and Harry, your brother['s] man, were both at Evesham this day sennight, and, as I heard, bestow 20[li.] there in knit hose; wherefore I think you may do good, if you can have money.

(B) Extract from letter of Abraham Sturley to Richard Quyny in London, November 4, 1598. (Ibid.)

Your letter of the 25. of October came to my hands the last of the same at night per Greenway,[1] which imported a stay of suits by Sir Ed. Gr[eville's] advice, until &c.,[2] and that only you should follow on for

1 Greenway was the 'carrier' who delivered parcels between London and Stratford.
2 So in the original. Sir Edward Greville was lord of the manor of Stratford, with whom the town corporation frequently had trouble.

*tax and subsidy[1] presently, and also your travel and
hinderance of answer therein by your long travel and
the affairs of the Court; and that our countryman, Mr.
Wm. Shak. would procure us money, which I will like
of as I shall hear when, and where, and how; and I
pray let not go that occasion, if it may sort to any indifferent[2] conditions.*

NOTE. Richard Quyny was a mercer by occupation.
Hence his father's suggestion for using any residue of
the money borrowed from Shakespeare to stock his
shop. Sturley's letter indicates that Quyny had informed him that Shakespeare would procure them
money on the very day (October 25) on which Quyny
addressed his note to the poet. Fripp (*Richard Quyny,*
p. 139) assumes from this that Quyny must have received a favorable answer from the poet on the same
day; but Sturley is evidently uncertain about details
and somewhat skeptical.

XXIII. SHAKESPEARE SELLS A LOAD OF STONE TO THE STRATFORD CORPORATION (1599).

Stratford Chamberlains' Accounts, January 12,
1599.

Paid to Mr. Shaxspere for one load of stone x^d.

NOTE. It is conjectured that the stone was what was
left on Shakespeare's hands after repairing New Place,
which was in bad condition when the poet bought it.
The load of stone was used by the Stratford authorities to mend the bridge across the Avon.

1 'That you should confine yourself to securing from the court a
relief from taxation.' Bad harvests and two disastrous fires had
greatly impoverished the town of Stratford.
2 Reasonable.

XXIV. JOHN WEEVER'S SONNET TO SHAKE-SPEARE (1599).

Sonnet addressed 'Ad Gulielmum Shakespeare' in *Epigrams in the Oldest Cut and Newest Fashion.*

Honey-tongued Shakespeare, when I saw thine issue,
I swore Apollo got them and none other;
Their rosy-tainted features, clothed in tissue,
Some heavenborn goddess said to be their mother:
Rose-cheek'd Adonis with his amber tresses,
Fair, fire-hot Venus charming him to love her,
Chaste Lucretia virgin-like her dresses,
Proud lust-stung Tarquin seeking still to prove her:
Romeo, Richard, more whose names I know not,
Their sugar'd tongues and pure attractive beauty
Say they are Saints, although that Saints they show
    not,
For thousands vow to them subjective duty.
    They burn in love thy children. Shakespear, let
      them:
    Go, woo thy Muse more nymphish brood beget them.

XXV. SHAKESPEARE A PART OWNER OF THE GLOBE THEATRE (1599).

Reference to the newly erected Globe Theatre in post-mortem inventory (May 16, 1599) of the property of Sir Thomas Brend, whose son had leased the site of the building to Shakespeare and his partners.

Una domo de novo edificata . . . in occupacione Willielmi Shakespeare et aliorum.[1]

NOTE. When the Globe was built in 1599 a half-interest in the property was assigned to the brothers,

---

[1] '[In] a house newly built . . . in the occupation of W. Shakespeare and others.'

Richard and Cuthbert Burbage, and the remaining half-interest divided equally among five actors of the Chamberlain's Company: Shakespeare, Kempe, Pope, Phillips, and Heminge. Shakespeare, therefore, had at the start a one-tenth share in the theatre. The mathematical proportion of his interest to the entire property varied in later years as some of his fellow-sharers retired and new ones came in.

A later inventory of the Brend estate, in 1601, names the tenants of the playhouse as 'Richard Burbage and William Shackespeare, Gent.'—mentioning, that is, simply the two most famous of the sharers.

XXVI. CONFIRMATION AND EXTENSION OF HERALDIC HONORS TO JOHN SHAKESPEARE (1599).

Draft, prepared jointly by the two heralds, William Dethick and William Camden, confirming John Shakespeare's right to the arms previously granted and authorizing him to impale the Arden arms. (Heralds' College, London.)

To all and singular, noble and gentlemen, of all estates and degrees bearing arms, to whom these presents shall come, William Dethick, Garter-principal King of Arms of England, and William Camden, als [alias] Clarentieulx, King of Arms for the south, east, and west parts of this realm, sendeth greetings. Know ye that in all nations and kingdoms the record and remembrances of the valiant facts and virtuous dispositions of worthy men have been made known and divulged by certain shields of arms and tokens of chivalry, the grant and testimony whereof appertaineth unto us by virtue of our offices from the Queen's

most excellent majesty and her Highness' most noble
and victorious progenitors. Wherefore being solicited
and by credible report informed that John Shakespere,
now of Stratford-upon-Avon in the county of Warwick, gent., whose parent, great-grandfather, and late
antecessor for his faithful and approved service to the
late most prudent prince King H. 7. of famous memory
was advanced and rewarded with lands and tenements
given to him in those parts of Warwickshire, where
they have continued by some descents in good reputation and credit; and for that the said John Shakespere
having married the daughter and one of the heirs of
Robert Arden of Wellingcote in the said county and
also produced this his ancient coat of arms heretofore
assigned to him whilst he was her Majesty's officer
and bailiff of that town:—In consideration of the
premisses and for the encouragement of his posterity,
unto whom such blazon of arms and achievements of
inheritance from their said mother by the ancient
custom and laws of arms may lawfully descend, we
the said Garter and Clarentieulx have assigned,
granted, and confirmed, and by these presents exem-
plified, unto the said John Shakespere and to his posterity, that shield and coat of arms, viz., in a field of
gold upon a bend sables a spear of the first, the point
upward headed, argent; and for his crest or cognizance
a falcon with his wings displayed, standing on a
wreath of his colors, supporting a spear headed or
and steeled silver, fixed upon a helmet with mantels
and tassels as more plainly may appear depicted on
this margent. And we have likewise upon another
escutcheon impaled the same with the ancient arms
of the said Arden of Wellingcote, signifying thereby
that it may and shall be lawful for the said John Shake-

spere, gent. to bear and use the same shields of arms, single or impaled as aforesaid, during his natural life, and that it shall be lawful for his children, issue, and posterity (lawfully begotten) to bear, use, and quarter, and show forth the same with their due differences in all lawful warlike facts and civil use or exercises, according to the laws of arms and custom that to gent[lemen] belongeth, without let or interruption of any person or persons for use or per[1] bearing the same. In witness and testimony whereof we have subscribed our names and fastened the seals of our offices. Given at the Office of Arms, London, the .[2] . . in the xlii[to] year of the reign of our most gracious Sovereign, Elizabeth by the grace of God [Queen of England, France] and Ireland, Defender of the faith, &c. 1599.

NOTE. See document XIII for Dethick's earlier grant of arms to John Shakespeare. William Camden, the famous antiquary, who is associated with Dethick in the present document, had been made Clarenceux herald in 1597, after the date of Dethick's first drafts.

XXVII. SHAKESPEARE'S NAME EXPLOITED BY W. JAGGARD (1599).

Title-page of a collection of short poems by various authors.

THE PASSIONATE PILGRIM. By W. Shakespeare. At London. Printed for W. Jaggard . . . 1599.

---

1 The manuscript has 'per bearing,' which may, however, be a slip for 'forbearing.'

2 The precise date of the present paper is uncertain because of a tear in the paper at this point; but as Elizabeth's 42d regnal year did not begin till November 17, 1599, it was evidently late in the calendar year, 1599, or in the period, Jan. 1-Mar. 24, 1600.

NOTE. This small pamphlet contained twenty poems, of which five were by Shakespeare. All were doubtless secured more or less dishonestly by Jaggard, and his attribution of the whole work to Shakespeare on the title-page is, as Munro says (*Shakspere Allusion Book,* i. 63) 'a testimony to the market-value of Shakspere's name.' The book reached a third edition in 1612, and Jaggard had the further effrontery to increase the small size of this by inserting (still under Shakespeare's name) two long poems by Thomas Heywood, filched from the latter poet's *Britain's Troy.* Heywood protested in the following words, affixed to his *Apology for Actors* in the same year (1612):

'Here likewise I must necessarily insert a manifest injury done me in that work,[1] by taking the two Epistles of Paris to Helen and Helen to Paris and printing them in a less volume,[2] under the name of another,[3] which may put the world in opinion I might steal them from him[3]; and he to do himself right hath since published them in his own name: but as I must acknowledge my lines not worthy his patronage, under whom[3] he hath published them, so the author[3] I know much offended with M. Jaggard that (altogether unknown to him) presumed to make so bold with his name.'

XXVIII. FIRST MENTION OF SHAKESPEARE'S NAME IN REGISTER OF THE STATIONERS' COMPANY (1600).

Transcript of Stationers' Register (copyright notice of *Much Ado about Nothing* and *2 Henry IV*).

---

1 I.e. *Britain's Troy,* of which Jaggard had also been the publisher.
2 I.e. *The Passionate Pilgrim,* 3d edition.
3 I.e. Shakespeare.

*1600 23 Augusti Andrew Wise William Aspley
Entered for their copies under the hands of the wardens two books, the one called Much Ado about Nothing, the other the second part of the History of King
Henry the IIII*[th], *with the humors of Sir John Falstaff,
written by Master Shakespere.*

XXIX. SHAKESPEARE'S FAME EXTENDS TO CAMBRIDGE (1600).

Allusions in the First Part of *The Return from Parnassus*, a student comedy, representing under-graduate life at Cambridge.

We shall have nothing but pure Shakspeare and shreds of poetry that he hath gathered at the theatres. (Ll. 1009 f.)

Mark, Romeo and Juliet! O monstrous theft! (L. 1015.)

Gullio, an affected poetaster, recites six lines of *Venus and Adonis,* and Ingenioso remarks: *Sweet Mr. Shakspeare!* (Ll. 1018-24.)

Gullio asks Ingenioso to write a poem for him—

Ingen. My pen is your bounden vassal to command. But what vein would it please you to have them in?

Gull. Not in a vain vein (pretty, i' faith!): make me them in two or three divers veins—in Chaucer's, Gower's, and Spenser's and Mr. Shakespeare's. Marry, I think I shall entertain those verses which run like these:

*Even as the sun with purple colour'd face
Had ta'en his last leave on the weeping morn, &c.*[1]
O sweet Mr. Shakspeare! I'le have his picture in my study at the court. (Ll. 1048-55.)

1 Opening lines of *Venus and Adonis,* slightly misquoted.

Later Gullio says, *Let me hear Mr. Shakspear's vein;* and Ingenioso recites seven lines in imitation of *Venus and Adonis.* Gullio says:

No more! I am one that can judge according to the proverb, 'bovem ex unguibus.' Ay, marry, Sir, these have some life in them! Let this duncified world esteem of Spenser and Chaucer, I'll worship sweet Mr. Shakspeare, and to honour him will lay his Venus and Adonis under my pillow, as we read of one (I do not well remember his name, but I am sure he was a king) slept with Homer under his bed's head. (Ll. 1211-27.)

XXX. SHAKESPEARE AND HIS WIFE MENTIONED IN THOMAS WHITTINGTON'S WILL (1601).

Extract from the will of Thomas Whittington of Shottery, who died in April, 1601, bequeathing

Unto the poor people of Stratford xl s. that is in the hand of Anne Shaxspere, wife unto Mr. William Shaxspere, and is due debt unto me, being paid to mine executor by the said William Shaxspere or his assigns according to the true meaning of this my will.

NOTE. Whittington was a shepherd who had been in the employ of the Hathway family. It has been sentimentally supposed that he assisted the poet's wife with a loan of forty shillings at some long past period of embarrassment, while Shakespeare was absent in London. It is equally likely that the sum had been entrusted to the Shakespeares for safe keeping or represented a promised gratuity or uncollected wages.

See J. W. Gray, *Shakespeare's Marriage,* 28, 29.

XXXI. DEATH OF SHAKESPEARE'S FATHER (1601).

Stratford Burial Register.

1601 Septemb. 8 Mr. Johannes Shakspeare.

NOTE. On his father's death the poet, as eldest son, inherited the double house in Henley Street in which he had been born. His mother continued to live there until her death, as did also his married sister, Mrs. Joan Hart, and her family.

XXXII. A CAMBRIDGE ANECDOTE OF SHAKESPEARE AND BEN JONSON (1601-1602).

From the Second Part of *The Return from Parnassus*, acted at Cambridge, probably in December, 1601, or January, 1602. One scene (IV. v.) represents Shakespeare's actor colleagues, Kempe and Burbage coming to Cambridge to get student recruits for their company. They talk together:

Kempe. Few of the university pen plays well. They smell too much of that writer, Ovid, and that writer, Metamorphosis, and talk too much of Proserpina and Jupiter. Why, here's our fellow Shakespeare puts them all down; ay, and Ben Jonson too. O that Ben Jonson is a pestilent fellow: he brought up Horace giving the poets a pill, but our fellow Shakespeare hath given him a purge that made him beray his credit.

Burbage. It is a shrewd fellow indeed . . .

NOTE. Kempe left Shakespeare's company (the Lord Chamberlain's) in 1600, and joined Worcester's Men in 1602. The passage refers to the so-called 'War of

the Theatres' in 1601. The play by Jonson alluded
to is *Poetaster,* of that year, in which Horace gives
Marston-Crispinus a pill. What the purge that Shakespeare gave Jonson was has been much disputed. It
was probably something in the early version of *Hamlet,* acted at Cambridge in 1601, which was omitted in
the printed editions.

XXXIII. JOHN MANNINGHAM'S ANECDOTE OF SHAKESPEARE AND BURBAGE (1602).

From the diary of John Manningham, a barrister
of the Middle Temple, London, March 13, 1602.
(British Museum, MS. Room.)

*Upon a time when Burbage played Richard the
Third there was a citizen grew so far in liking with
him, that before she went from the play she appointed
him to come that night unto her by the name of Richard
the Third. Shakespeare, overhearing their conclu-
sion, went before, was entertained and at his game
ere Burbage came. Then message being brought that
Richard the Third was at the door, Shakespeare
caused return to be made that William the Conqueror
was before Richard the Third. Shakespeare's name
William.*

XXXIV. SHAKESPEARE BUYS A LARGE TRACT OF ARABLE LAND IN OLD STRAT-FORD (1602).

Conveyance of one hundred and seven acres from
William and John Combe to Shakespeare, May 1,
1602. (Shakespeare Birthplace Museum.)

*This indenture made the first day of May, in the
four-and-fortieth year of the reign of our Sovereign*

Lady, Elizabeth, by the grace of God of England, France and Ireland Queen, Defendress of the Faith, &c., between William Combe of Warwick in the county of Warwick, Esquire, and John Combe of Old Stratford, in the county aforesaid, Gentleman, on the one party, and William Shakespere of Stretford-upon-Avon, in the county aforesaid, Gentleman, on the other party, Witnesseth that the said William Combe and John Combe, for and in consideration of the sum of three hundred and twenty pounds of current English money to them in hand, at and before the ensealing and delivery of these presents, well and truly satisfied, contented, and paid, whereof and wherewith they acknowledge themselves fully satisfied, contented, and paid, and thereof and of every part and parcel thereof do clearly exonerate, acquit, and discharge the said William Shakespere, his heirs, executors, administrators, and assigns for ever by these presents, have aliened, bargained, sold, given, granted, and confirmed, and by these presents do fully, clearly and absolutely alien, bargain, sell, give, grant, and confirm unto the said William Shakespere all and singular those arable lands, with the appurtenances, containing by estimation four yardland of arable land, situate, lying, and being within the parish, fields or town of Old Stretford aforesaid, in the said county of Warwick, containing by estimation one hundred and seven acres, be they more or less; and also all the common of pasture for sheep, horse, kine, or other cattle in the fields of Old Stretford aforesaid, to the said four yardland belonging or in any wise appertaining; and also all hades, leys, tyings, profits, advantages and commodities whatsoever, with their and every of their appurtenances to the said bargained premises belonging or appertaining, or heretofore reputed, taken, known, or occupied as part, parcel, or member of the same, and the reversion and reversions of all and singular the same bargained premises, and of every part and parcel thereof, now or late in the several tenures or occupations of Thomas Hiccoxe and Lewes Hiccoxe, or of either of them, or of their assigns, or any of them; together also with all charters, deeds, writings, escripts, and muniments whatsoever touching or concerning the same premises only, or only any part or parcel thereof; and also the true copies of all other deeds, evidences, charters, writings, escripts, and muniments which do touch and concern the said premises before bargained and sold, or any part or parcel thereof, which the said William Combe or John Combe now have in their custody or hereafter may have, or which they may lawfully get or come by without suit in law; to have and to hold the said four yard of arable land, containing by estimation one hundred and seven acres, be they more or less, and all and singular other the premises before by these presents aliened and sold, or mentioned or intended to be aliened and sold and every part and parcel thereof; and all deeds, charters, writings, escripts, and muniments, before by these presents bargained and sold unto the said William Shakespere, his heirs and assigns for ever, to the only proper use and behoof of the said William Shakespere, his heirs and assigns for ever. . . .[1] In witness whereof the parties to these presents have interchangeably set their hands and seals, the day and year first above written, 1602.—W. Combe.— Jo. Combe.—Sealed and delivered to Gilbert Shake-

---

1 The document contains nearly a thousand words more of legal redundancy. For the omitted section see Halliwell-Phillipps, *Outlines*, 1887, ii. 17-19.

spere, to the use of the within-named William Shake-
spere, in the presence of Anthony Nashe, William
Sheldon, Humfrey Mainwaring, Richard Mason, John
Nashe.

NOTE. Gilbert Shakespeare was the poet's younger
brother, born in 1566, evidently acting because the
actual purchaser was unable to leave London. On
March 5, 1610, he witnessed a deed in Stratford. He
was probably the 'Gilbertus Shakspeare, adolescens'
buried, according to the Stratford Register, February
3, 1612. (See no. LV, and Mrs. Stopes, *Shakespeare's
Environment,* pp. 63 ff., 332 ff.)

XXXV. SHAKESPEARE GETS ASSURANCE OF HIS TITLE TO NEW PLACE FROM HERCULES UNDERHILL (1602).

Foot of second 'fine' levied on New Place, Michaelmas, 1602. (Public Record Office.)

Inter Willielmum Shakespeare, generosum, queren-
tem, et Herculem Underhill, generosum, deforciantem,
de uno mesuagio, duobus horreis, duobus gardinis, et
duobus pomariis cum pertinenciis, in Stretford-super-
Avon . . . et pro hac recognicione, remissione, quieta
clamancia, warantia, fine et concordia idem Willielmus
dedit predicto Herculi sexaginta libras sterlingorum.

NOTE. This document agrees verbally with the 'fine'
which Shakespeare received from William Underhill in
1597 (see document XV), except for the addition of
two orchards (duobus pomariis) not mentioned in the
earlier paper and the substitution of Hercules Underhill in place of his deceased father, William, as deforciant. Halliwell-Phillipps (*Outlines,* 7th ed., i.

204) explains that some flaw had been discovered in
Shakespeare's title to the property. 'In order to meet
this difficulty it was necessary for a fine to be levied
through which the absolute ownership of the purchaser
should be recognized by Hercules, and of so much importance was this considered that, upon the deforciant
representing in June, 1602, that the state of his health
prevented his undertaking a journey to London, a
special commission was arranged for obtaining his
acknowledgment. This important ratification was
procured in Northamptonshire in the following October, Shakespeare no doubt being responsible for the
considerable expenditure that must have been incurred
by these transactions.' The strange facts that ac-
counted for the second deed were discovered by Mrs.
Stopes (*Shakespeare's Warwickshire Contemporaries,*
231 f.). William Underhill was poisoned by his elder
son, Fulke, a few months after the sale of New Place
to Shakespeare, dying July 7, 1597. His property
finally passed to his younger son, Hercules, who came
of age in 1602, when Shakespeare found it desirable
to get assurance of his title.

XXXVI. SHAKESPEARE BUYS A COTTAGE AND LAND OPPOSITE NEW PLACE (1602).

(A) Record in the court rolls of the manor of Rowington of surrender of title by Walter Getley to Shakespeare, September 28, 1602. (Shakespeare Birthplace
Museum.)

*Rowington.—Visus franci plegii cum curia baronis
prenobilis domine Anne, Comitisse Warwici, ibidem
tentus vicesimo octavo die Septembris, anno regni
domine nostre Elizabethe, Dei gracia Anglie, Francie*

et Hibernie regine, fidei defensoris, etc., quadrigesimo quarto, coram Henrico Michell, generoso, deputato scenescallo Johannis Huggeford, armigeri, capitalis scenescalli ibidem. Ad hanc curiam venit Walterus Getley, per Thomam Tibbottes, juniorem, attornatum suum, unum customariorum tenencium manerii predicti, predicto Thoma Tibbottes jurato pro veritate inde, et sursum reddidit in manus domine manerii predicti unum cotagium, cum pertinenciis, scituatum, jacens et existens in Stratford-super-Avon, in quodam vico ibidem vocato Walkers Streete alias Dead Lane, ad opus et usum Willielmi Shackespere et heredum suorum imperpetuum, secundum consuetudinem manerii predicti; et sic remanet in manibus domine manerii predicti, quousque predictus Willielmus Shakespere venerit ad capiendum premissa predicta. In cujus rei testimonium predictus Henricus Michell huic presenti copie sigullum suum apposuit die et anno supradictis. —Per me, Henricum Michell.[1]

(B) From survey of customary tenants and rents in Manor of Rowington (1603-1604).

In Stratford, parcel of the Manor there . . . William Shakespere likewise holdeth one cottage and one

[1] 'View of frank pledge, with the court baron of the noble Lady, Anne Countess of Warwick, held in the same place on the 28th day of September in the 44th year of the reign of our lady Elizabeth . . . before Henry Michell, Gent., deputy seneschal for John Huggeford, Esq., chief seneschal there. To this court came Walter Getley through his attorney, Thos. Tibbotts, Jr., one of the customary tenants of the aforesaid manor, the aforesaid T. Tibbotts being put on oath, and he restored into the hands of the lady of the aforesaid manor a cottage, with its appurtenances, situated, lying, and existing in Stratford-on-Avon, in a certain street there called Walker's St. or Dead Lane, to the benefit and use of Wm. Shackespere and his heirs forever, according to the custom of the aforesaid manor; and so it remains in the hands of the lady of the aforesaid manor till the aforesaid W. Shakespere shall come to receive the aforesaid premises. In testimony of which the aforesaid H. Michell has affixed his seal to the present copy on the day and year aforesaid. By me, Henry Michell.'

garden by estimation a quarter of an acre and payeth rent yearly 2s. 6d.

[Also a similar note in a survey dated Aug. 1, 1606, which gives the yearly nominal rent as 2s.]

NOTE. Shakespeare thus acquired a 'copyhold' title in accordance with old feudal law, the property in question being held as part of the Manor of Rowington, of which the Countess of Warwick, widow of Ambrose Earl of Warwick, was lady of the manor. The property consisted of a quarter acre of land with a cottage, facing the lower grounds of New Place and standing on Chapel Lane (formerly called Walker's Street). Shakespeare secured possession of the property, which he bequeathed to his daughter Susanna. For further details see Mrs. Stopes, 'Shakespeare, Homager of Rowington' in *Shakespeare's Industry,* pp. 267 ff.

XXXVII. SHAKESPEARE AND HIS COLLEAGUES BECOME THE KING'S SERVANTS (1603).

James I's instructions to his Keeper of the Privy Seal, endorsed 'The Players' Privilege,' May 17, 1603. (Public Record Office.)

By the King. Right trusty and well beloved counselor, we greet you well, and will and command you that under our Privy Seal in your custody for the time being you cause our letters to be directed to the Keeper of our Great Seal of England, commanding him that under our said Great Seal he cause our letters to be made patents in form following:—James, by the grace of God King of England, Scotland, France

and Ireland, Defender of the Faith, &c., to all justices,
mayors, sheriffs, constables, headboroughs, and other
our officers and loving subjects, greeting. Know ye
that we, of our special grace, certain knowledge, and
mere motion, have licensed and authorized, and by
these presents do license and authorize, these our
servants, Lawrence Fletcher, William Shakespeare,
Richard Burbage, Augustine Phillippes, John Hen-
ninges, Henry Condell, William Sly, Robert Armyn,
Richard Cowlye, and the rest of their associates,
freely to use and exercise the art and faculty of playing comedies, tragedies, histories, interludes, morals,
pastorals, stage-plays, and such other, like as they have
already studied or hereafter shall use or study, as well
for the recreation of our loving subjects as for our
solace and pleasure when we shall think good to see
them, during our pleasure. And the said comedies,
tragedies, histories, interludes, moral[s], pastorals,
stage-plays, and such like to show and exercise publicly to their best commodity, when the infection of
the plague shall decrease, as well within their now
usual house called the Globe, within our county of
Surrey, as also within any townhalls or motehalls or
other convenient places within the liberties and free-
dom of any other city, university, town, or borough
whatsoever within our said realms and dominions,
willing and commanding you and every of you, as you
tender our pleasure, not only to permit and suffer them
herein without any your lets, hindrances, or molesta-
tions during our said pleasure, but also to be aiding
and assisting to them, if any wrong be to them offered,
and to allow them such former courtesies as hath been
given to men of their place and quality. And also what

*further favor you shall show to these our servants for
our sake we shall take kindly at your hands. In witness whereof &c. And these our letters shall be your
sufficient warrant and discharge in this behalf. Given
under our signet at our manor of Greenwich the
seventeenth day of May in the first year of our reign
of England, France, and Ireland, and of Scotland the
six-and-thirtieth.—Ex: per Lake.[1]—To our right trusty
and well beloved counselor, the Lord Cecill of Esing-
don, Keeper of our Privy Seal for the time being.*

NOTE. The royal patent here called for was formally
issued two days later, the language being virtually
the same. The significance of this emphatic testimonial of royal favor is enhanced by the circumstance
that James had arrived in London to begin his reign
only ten days before (May 7).

Lawrence Fletcher, who here first appears as a colleague of Shakespeare, had acted before King James
in Scotland in 1599 and again in 1601.

XXXVIII. CAMDEN RANKS SHAKESPEARE AMONG THE ENGLISH IMMORTALS (1603).

From William Camden's survey of English poetry
in his *Remains of a Greater Work concerning Britain.*

*These may suffice for some poetical descriptions of
our ancient poets; if I would come to our time, what
a world could I present to you out of Sir Philip Sidney,
Ed. Spenser, Samuel Daniel, Hugh Holland, Ben.
Jonson, Th. Campion, Mich. Drayton, George Chapman, John Marston, William Shakespeare, and other*

---

1 Expedi ('put it into effect') per Lake. Thomas Lake, clerk of the
signet under Elizabeth; made Latin secretary to James and knighted,
1603; appointed keeper of the records at Whitehall, 1604.

most pregnant wits of these our times, whom succeeding ages may justly admire.

NOTE. This book of Camden was first printed in 1605, but the date attached to the dedicatory epistle, June 12, 1603, indicates that it was complete in manuscript at the earlier period. For Camden's interest in Shakespeare's heraldic ambitions see no. XXVI.

XXXIX. GRANT OF RED CLOTH TO SHAKE-SPEARE AS GROOM OF THE KING'S CHAMBER IN JAMES I'S CORONATION PROCESSION (1604).

From the accounts of the Master of the Wardrobe, March 15, 1604. (Public Record Office.)

The Accompt of Sir George Hume, Knight, Master of the great Wardrobe to the high and mighty Prince, our Gracious Sovereign Lord, James by the Grace of God King of England, Scotland, France, & Ireland, Defender of the Faith, &c, as well of all his receipts as of his emptions and deliveries of all manner of furnitures and provisions whatsoever by him bought and provided for his Majesty's use and service against his royal entry and proceeding through his honorable city of London, together with our Sovereign Lady, Queen Anne, his wife, and the noble Prince Henry his son, solemnized the xv^{th} day of March, 1603 [i.e. 1604] and in the first year of his reign of England, France, & Ireland, & of Scotland the seven-and-thirtieth. . . . Red Cloth bought of sundry persons and given by his Majesty to divers persons against his Majesty's said royal proceeding through the City of London, viz.: . . . The Chamber . . .

		Red cloth
	William Shakespeare	iiij yards di.[1]
	Augustine Phillipps	iiij yards di.
	Lawrence Fletcher	iiij yards di.
	John Hemminges	iiij yards di.
Players	Richard Burbidge	iiij yards di.
	William Slye	iiij yards di.
	Robert Armyn	iiij yards di.
	Henry Cundell	iiij yards di.
	Richard Cowley	iiij yards di.

NOTE. The King's formal entry into London had been delayed for nearly a year by reason of the plague, which raged through the year 1603.

XL. THE KING'S PLAYERS AS GROOMS OF THE ROYAL CHAMBER IN ATTENDANCE ON THE SPANISH AMBASSADOR (1604).

From the Declared Accounts of the Treasurer of the King's Chamber, August, 1604. (Public Record Office.)

To Augustine Phillipps and John Hemynges for the allowance of themselves and ten of their fellows, his Majesty's Grooms of the Chamber and Players, for waiting and attending on his Majesty's service by commandment upon the Spanish Ambassador at Somerset House, for the space of 18 days; viz., from the 9th day of August, 1604, until the 27th day of the same, as appeareth by a bill thereof signed by the Lord Chamberlain—21ll. 12s.

NOTE. Though Shakespeare's name is not specifically mentioned, it is virtually certain that he was included

1 Four yards and a half (dimidium).

among the ten 'fellows' of Phillips and Heminge. See Ernest Law, *Shakespeare as a Groom of the Chamber,* 1910, and compare the lists of nine King's Players in documents XXXVII and XXXIX.

XLI. ANTHONY SCOLOKER ON 'FRIENDLY SHAKESPEARE' AND HIS HAMLET (1604).

Epistle prefatory to *Daiphantus, or the Passions of Love,* 1604.

It should be like the never-too-well-read Arcadia . . . or to come home to the vulgar's element like Friendly Shakespeare's tragedies, where the comedian rides when the tragedian stands on tiptoe: 'faith it should please all, like Prince Hamlet.

XLII. THE KING'S MEN PERFORM SHAKE-SPEARE'S PLAYS AT COURT (1604-1605).

Extracts from the Revels Accounts. (Public Record Office.)

The Revels Book. Anno 1605. The Accompt of the Office of the Revels of this whole year's charge in anno 1604, until the last of October, 1605.

The Players	1604	The poets which made the plays
By the King's Majesty's Players	Hallowmas Day, being the first of November, a play in the banqueting house at Whitehall, called The Moor of Venice.	
By his Majesty's Players	The Sunday following a play of The Merry Wives of Windsor.	

The Players	1604	The poets which made the plays
By his Majesty's Players	On St. Stephen's Night [Dec. 26] in the Hall a play called Measure for Measure.	Shaxberd
	. . . .	
By his Majesty's Players	On Innocents' Night [Dec. 28] the Play of Errors.	Shaxberd
	. . . . . .	
By his Majesty's Players	Between New Year's Day and Twelfth Day [Jan. 6] a play of Love's Labour's Lost.	
	. . . . . .	
By his Majesty's Players	On the 7 of January was played the play of Henry the Fift[h].	
	. . . . . .	
By his Majesty's Players	On Shrove Sunday a play of the Merchant of Venice.	Shaxberd
	. . . . . .	
By his Majesty's Players	On Shrove Tuesday a play called the Merchant of Venice, again commanded by the King's Majesty.	Shaxberd

NOTE. These notices, discovered by Peter Cunningham in 1842, were branded as 'unquestionably a modern forgery' by Halliwell-Phillipps, who however admits that the facts they record are otherwise confirmed and probably true. There is a strong probability at present in favor of the genuineness of the document. The strange spelling (e.g. in *Shaxberd*) is doubtless owing to the fact that the paper was written by a newly arrived Scot.

XLIII. BEQUEST OF A GOLD PIECE TO SHAKESPEARE FROM AUGUSTINE PHILLIPS (1605).

From the will of Augustine Phillips of the King's Company, May 4, 1605. (Somerset House, London.)

Item, I give and bequeath to my fellow, William Shakespeare, a thirty shillings piece in gold; to my fellow, Henry Condell, one other thirty shilling piece in gold; to my servant, Christopher Beeston, thirty shillings in gold; to my fellow, Lawrence Fletcher, twenty shillings in gold; to my fellow, Robert Armin, twenty shillings in gold; to my fellow, Richard Cowley, twenty shillings in gold; to my fellow, Alexander Cook, twenty shillings in gold; to my fellow, Nicholas Tooley, twenty shillings in gold.

XLIV. SHAKESPEARE PURCHASES AN INTEREST IN THE TITHES OF STRATFORD AND ADJACENT VILLAGES (1605).

Essential sections of deed from Ralph Huband to William Shakespeare, July 24, 1605. (Shakespeare Birthplace Museum.)

This indenture made the four-and-twentieth day of July in the years of the reign of our Sovereign Lord, James . . . that is to say, of England, France, and Ireland the third, and of Scotland the eight-and-thirtieth, between Raphe Hubande of Ippesley in the county of Warwick, Esq., on the one part, and William Shakespear of Stratford-upon-Avon in the said county of Warwick, Gent., on the other part. . . .

This indenture now witnesseth that the said Raphe Hubande, for and in consideration of the sum of four hundred and forty pounds of lawful English money

to him by the said *William Shakespear* before the ensealing and delivery of these presents well and truly
contented and paid, whereof and of every part and
parcel whereof he, the said *Raphe Hubande,* doth by
these presents acknowledge the receipt, and thereof
and of every part and parcel thereof doth clearly
acquit, exonerate, and discharge the said *William
Shakespear,* his executors and administrators, for
ever by these presents—hath demised, granted, assigned, and set over, and by these presents doth demise, grant, assign, and set over unto the said *William
Shakespear,* his executors and assigns, the moiety or
one-half of all and singular the said tithes of corn,
grain, blade, and hay, yearly and from time to time
coming, increasing, renewing, arising, growing, issuing, or happening, or to be had, received, perceived, or
taken out of, upon, or in the towns, villages, hamlets,
grounds, and fields of *Stratford, Old Stratford, Welcombe,* and *Bushopton* aforesaid in the said county of
Warwick, and also the moiety or one-half of all and
singular the said tithes of wool, lamb, and other small
and privy tithes, herbage, oblations, obventions, al-
terages, muniments, and offerings whatsoever. . . .

  To have and to hold all and every the said moieties
or one-half of all and singular the said tithes before in
and by these presents lastly mentioned to be granted
and assigned . . . unto the said *William Shakespear,*
his executors and assigns, from the day of the date
hereof, for and during the residue of the said term of
fourscore and twelve years in the said first recited indenture mentioned, and for such and so long term and
time, and in as large, ample, and beneficial manner as
the said *Raphe Hubande* should or ought enjoy the
same, yielding and paying therefor yearly during the

*residue of the said term of fourscore and twelve years
which be yet to come and unexpired, the rents hereafter mentioned, in manner and form following: that
is to say, unto the bailiff and burgesses of Stratford
aforesaid, and their successors, the yearly rent of
seventeen pounds at the feasts of St. Michael the Arch-
angel and the Annunciation of blessed Mary the Virgin
by equal portions, and unto the said John Barker, his
executors, administrators, or assigns, the annual or
yearly rent of five pounds. . . . And the said William
Shakespear doth by these presents, for him, his heirs,
executors, and administrators, covenant and grant to
and with the said Raphe Hubande, his executors, administrators, and assigns that he, the said William
Shakespear, his executors, administrators, or assigns,
shall and will, during the residue of the said term
of fourscore and twelve years which be yet to come
and unexpired, yearly content and pay the several
rents abovementioned, viz.; seventeen pounds to the
bailiff and burgesses of Stratford aforesaid, and five
pounds to the said John Barker, his executors or
assigns, at the days and places aforesaid in which it
ought to be paid according to the purport and true
meaning of these presents, and thereof shall and will
discharge the said Raphe Hubande, his executors, administrators, and assigns. In witness whereof the
parties abovesaid to these presents have set their seals
the day and year first above written.*

NOTE. The entire document, which runs to over four
thousand words, is printed by Halliwell-Phillipps,
Outlines, 7th ed., ii. 19-25. The original lease of the
tithe estate for 92 years had been made in 1544 by a
since extinct ecclesiastical corporation, the College or
Collegiate Church of Stratford. When Shakespeare

bought his interest in it, the lease still had thirty-one years to run, after which the property reverted to the corporation of Stratford.

The nature of the 'moiety or one-half' interest that Shakespeare bought from Huband seems usually to be misunderstood. It was not half the entire tithe property as originally leased by the 'College'—an immensely large and miscellaneous set of holdings—but half of certain specified kinds of tithes in certain of the villages concerned. The other 'moiety' of this property belonged to the Combe family, but would pass in 1613 to Shakespeare's cousin and legal adviser, Thomas Greene. These facts appear in the later document of 1609. See no. LI, p. 60.

XLV. MARRIAGE OF SHAKESPEARE'S DAUGHTER SUSANNA (1607).

Stratford Marriage Register.

1607 Junij 5 John Hall, gentleman, and Susanna Shaxspere.

NOTE. John Hall, a learned man and distinguished physician, died in 1635 and his widow in 1649. They resided in New Place after the poet's death.

XLVI. SHAKESPEARE AT THE HEIGHT OF HIS FAME AS A DRAMATIST (1607).

Entry of *King Lear* in the Stationers' Register, November 26, 1607.

1607, 5 Regis 26 Nov. Na[thaniel] *Butter, Jo*[hn] *Burby entered for their copy, under the hands of Sir George Buck, Knight, and the wardens, a book called Mr. William Shakespeare his history of King Lear, as*

*it was played before the King's majesty at Whitehall
upon St. Stephen's Night* [Dec. 26] *at Christmas last
by his Majesty's Servants, playing usually at the Globe
on the Bankside.*

NOTE. This is quoted for the evidence it gives of the
importance which the publishers attached to Shakespeare's name on a play. *King Lear* was printed in
1608 with a title-page which similarly plays up the
poet's name:

*M. William Shak-speare: His True Chronicle His-
tory of the Life and Death of King Lear and his three
Daughters. With the unfortunate life of Edgar, son
and heir to the Earl of Gloster, and his sullen and
assumed humor of Tom of Bedlam: As it was played
before the King's Majesty at Whitehall upon St.
Stephen's Night in Christmas Holidays, by his Majesty's Servants playing usually at the Globe on the
Bankside.*

XLVII. BURIAL OF EDMUND, SHAKE-SPEARE'S BROTHER (1607).

Entries in burial register, St. Saviour's Church,
Southwark, December 31, 1607.

*1607 Decemb. 31 Edmond Shakespeare, a player,
in the Church.*

*Burials, December, 1607. 31. Edmund Shakspeare,
a player, buried in the Church with a forenoon knell
of the great bell, xx s.* (Sexton's Note.)

NOTE. St. Saviour's was the church nearest the Globe
Theatre; in it the dramatists Fletcher and Massinger
were later buried. Edmund Shakespeare was in his
twenty-eighth year when he died. He appears to have

attained no distinction as a player, but the records above indicate that he was interred with unusual dignity and expense.

XLVIII. BAPTISM OF SHAKESPEARE'S GRANDDAUGHTER (1608).

Stratford Baptismal Register.

1607 [i.e. 1608] *Februar. 21 Elizabeth, daughter to John Hall, gen.*

NOTE. This, Shakespeare's only granddaughter, was his last lineal descendant to survive. She lived till 1670 in honor and prosperity. See note on no. III.

XLIX. BURIAL OF SHAKESPEARE'S MOTHER (1608).

Stratford Burial Register.

1608 Sept. 9. Mary Shaxspere, widow.

NOTE. Evidence that Shakespeare probably returned to Stratford for this funeral has been found in the fact that he was godfather to William Walker, who was baptized in the Stratford Church shortly afterwards (Oct. 19). See allusion to 'my godson, William Walker,' in the poet's will (p. 84). But the argument is not strong.

L. SHAKESPEARE'S SUIT AGAINST JOHN ADDENBROOKE OF STRATFORD (1608-1609).

Series of seven legal papers in Latin dealing with Shakespeare's proceedings against Addenbrooke for

recovery of a debt of £6 in the Stratford court.[1]
(Stratford Court of Record.)

(A) Aug. 17, 1608. Warrant to the officers of the
court to bring the body of *Johannem Addenbrooke,
generosum*, into the next court of record, *ad respon-
dendum Willielmo Shackspeare, generoso, de placito
debiti.*[2] Endorsed: *Virtute istius precepti cepi in-
franominatum Johannem, cujus corpus paratum habeo
prout interius mihi precipitur. Manucaptor pro de-
fendente, Thomas Hornebye. Gilbertus Charnock,
serviens.*[3]

(B, C) December 21, 1608. Papers relating to
summons of jurymen to try the case of Shakespeare vs.
Addenbrooke.

(D, E) February 15, 1609. Note that the jurors de-
cide in favor of the plaintiff.

(F) March 15, 1609. Order citing John Addenbrooke before the next court of record *ad satisfacien-
dum Willielmo Shackspeare, generoso, tam de sex
libris debiti quas predictus Willielmus in eadem curia
versus eum recuperavit quam de viginti et quattuor
solidis qui ei adjudicati fuerunt pro dampnis et custa-
giis suis quos sustinuit occasione detentionis debiti
predicti.*[4] Endorsed: *Infranominatus Johannes non*

---

1 These documents are given in full by Halliwell-Phillipps, *Outlines*, 7th ed., ii. 78-80.
2 'To answer William Shackspeare, gentleman, in an action for
debt.'
3 'By virtue of this order I arrested the below-named John, whose
body I hold ready as is commanded to me within. Surety for the
defendant, Thomas Hornebye. (Signed) Gilbert Charnock, process-
server.'
4 'To satisfy William Shackspeare, gentleman, both for the six
pounds of debt which the aforesaid William recovered against him
in the same court and also for the twenty-four shillings which were
decreed to him for his damages and injuries which he sustained by
reason of the detention of the aforesaid debt.'

est inventus infra libertatem hujus burgi. Franciscus Boyce, serviens.[1]

(G) June 7, 1609. Order issued against Thomas Horneby to show cause why he should not, as surety for the defaulting Addenbrooke, pay Shakespeare the six pounds and twenty-four shillings which the court had awarded to the latter. Endorsement showing that the notice has been served on Horneby.

LI. COMPLAINT OF SHAKESPEARE AND OTHERS TO THE LORD CHANCELLOR REGARDING THE STRATFORD TITHES (1609).[2]

Stratford Corporation Records.

To the Right Honorable Thomas Lord Ellesmere, Lord Chancellor of England. In humble wise complaining shewen unto your honorable good Lordship your daily orators, Richard Lane of Awston in the county of Warwick, Esq., Thomas Greene of Stratford-upon-Avon in the said county of Warwick, Esq., and William Shackspeare of Stratford-upon-Avon aforesaid in the county of Warwick, gentleman . . . [A very elaborate document reciting the intricate history of the lease of Stratford tithes, interests in which are held by some forty different persons besides the three complainants. The entire property is subject to a yearly rent of 27 *l*. 13 *s*. 4 *d*. to John Barker's assignee, Henry Barker, who will be legally entitled to recover possession if any part of this is unpaid. Shakespeare's holding—about an eighth of the entire property—is by his deed charged with £5 as his contribu-

---

1 'The below-named John has not been found within the liberties of this borough.'
2 See 'Shakespeare's Moiety of the Stratford Tithes,' *Modern Language Notes,* Dec., 1925.

tion toward Barker's rent, and the same amount is charged against the other half-portion of Shakespeare's particular tithes held by the Combe family, and to which Thomas Greene has a reversionary title that will become effective in 1613; but the Combes decline to pay. In the cases of the other three dozen-odd persons concerned no agreement concerning the quota to be paid by each toward Barker's rent has been arrived at, and certain lawless spirits among them—notably Lord Carewe of Clopton—use their influence to dissuade anyone from paying at all.]

So as your orators their said respective estates and interests of and in their said several premises aforesaid, and the estates of divers of the said parties, which would gladly pay a reasonable part towards the said rent, but do now refuse to join with your said orators in this their said suit for fear of some other of the said parties which do so refuse to contribute, do remain and stand subject to be forfeited by the negligence or wilfulness of divers or any other of the said parties, which many times will pay nothing, whenas your orators Richard Lane and William Shackspeare, and some few others of the said parties, are wholly and against all equity and good conscience usually driven to pay the same for preservation of their estates of and in the parts of the premises belonging unto them; and albeit your said orators have taken great pains and travail in entreating and endeavoring to bring the said parties of their own accords and without suit of law to agree every one to a reasonable contribution toward the same residue of the said rent of xxvij li. xiij s. iiij d., according to the value of such of the premises as they enjoy . . . yet have they refused and denied, and still do refuse and deny, to be per-

suaded or drawn thereunto. . . . In tender considera-
tion whereof, and for so much as it is against all
equity and reason that the estates of some that are
willing to pay a reasonable part toward the said resi-
due of the said rent of xxvij li. xiij s. iiij d., having
respect to the smallness of the values of the things
they do possess, should depend upon the carelessness
and frowardness or other practices of others, which
will not pay a reasonable part or anything at all
toward the same; and for that it is most agreeable to
all reason, equity, and good conscience that every per-
son, his executors and assigns, should be ratably
charged with a yearly portion toward the said residue
of the said rent, according to the yearly benefit he en-
joyeth or receiveth; and for that your orators have no
means, by the order or course of the common laws of
this realm, to enforce or compel any of the said parties
to yield any certain contribution toward the same,
and so are and still shall be remediless therein unless
they may be in that behalf relieved by your Lordship's
gracious clemency and relief to others in such like cases
extended. May it therefore please your good Lord-
ship, the premises considered, and it being also con-
sidered that very many poor people's estates are sub-
ject to be overthrown by breach of the condition
aforesaid, and thereby do depend upon the negligences,
wills or practices of others, and shall continue daily in
doubt to be turned out of doors with their wives and
families through the practice or wilfulness of such
others, to write your honorable letters unto the said
Lord Carewe, thereby requiring him to appear in the
High Court of Chancery to answer to the premises,
and to grant unto your said orators his Majesty's most
gracious writs of subpoena to be directed unto the said

Sir Edward Greville, Sir Edward Conway, and other the said parties before named, and to the said Henry Barker . . . thereby commanding them and every of them at a certain day and under a certain pain therein to be limited to be and personally appear before your good Lordship in his Highness' most honorable Court of Chancery, fully, perfectly, and directly to answer to all and every the premises, and to set forth the several yearly values of the several premises so by them enjoyed, and to show good cause why a commission should not be awarded forth of the said most honorable court for the examining of witnesses to the several values aforesaid, and for the assessing, taxing and rating thereof, that thereupon it may appear how much every of the said parties . . . ought in reason proportionably to pay for the same towards the said residue of the said yearly rent of xxvij li. xiij s. iiij d. . . . .

Endorsed: *Lane, Greene et Shakspeare contra W. Combe et alios respondentes.*

NOTE. This paper bears no date and is variously ascribed to the years between 1609 and 1612, but internal evidence indicates, I think, that it was drawn up between January and March, 1609. The document presents Shakespeare not only in a shrewd and foresighted, but also in a courageous and public-spirited attitude. There is little doubt that the tyrants of his native fields whom he was withstanding yielded and that an arrangement fairer to the poet and his associates was arrived at. There is an answer to the complaint by William Combe, one of the defendants, which is in conciliatory tone. He asserts that he does pay five pounds yearly as his share of the common rent on his moiety of the Old Stratford,

Bishopton, and Welcombe tithes, and offers to pay 6 *s.* 8 *d.* for certain other tithes he holds, which he thinks the Complainants are willing to accept. He asks that if the court orders him to pay this further sum, the other parties mentioned in the complaint shall be required to contribute ratably to Barker's rent.

LII. SHAKESPEARE CONFIRMS AND EXTENDS HIS PURCHASE OF LAND FROM THE COMBES (1610).

(Public Record Office, London.)

Inter Willielmum Shakespere, generosum, querentem, et Willielmum Combe, armigerum, et Johannem Combe, generosum, deforciantes, de centum et septem acris terre et viginti acris pasture, cum pertinenciis, in Old Stratford et Stratford-super-Avon; unde placitum convencionis summonitum fuit inter eos, etc., scilicet, quod predicti Willielmus Combe et Johannes recognoverunt predicta tenementa, cum pertinenciis, esse jus ipsius Willielmi Shakespere, ut illa que idem Willielmus habet de dono predictorum Willielmi Combe et Johannis, et illa remiserunt et quietumclamaverunt de ipsis Willielmo Combe et Johanne, et heredibus suis, predicto Willielmo Shakespere et heredibus suis imperpetuum. . . . Et pro hac, etc. idem Willielmus Shakespere dedit predictis Willielmo Combe et Johanni centum libras sterlingorum.[1]

NOTE. This conveyance confirms Shakespeare's title in the 107 acres of arable land for which he had paid the Combes £320 in May, 1602, and gives him title in twenty additional acres of pasture land. For the earlier document see no. XXXIV.

[1] This document follows the usual Latin wording employed in conveyances by 'fine.' See nos. XV and XXXV.

LIII. SHAKESPEARE PRAISED AS A COMPANION FOR A KING (ca. 1611).

Epigram by John Davies of Hereford in *The Scourge of Folly.*

To our English Terence, Mr. Will. Shake-speare.

Some say (good Will)—which I in sport do sing—
  Had'st thou not played some kingly parts in sport,
Thou hadst been a companion for a king,
  And been a king among the meaner sort.
Some others rail; but, rail as they think fit,
Thou hast no railing but a reigning wit;
And honesty thou sow'st, which they do reap,
So to increase their stock which they do keep.

LIV. FRANCIS BEAUMONT (?) IN PRAISE OF SHAKESPEARE'S LACK OF LEARNING.

      Here I would let slip
(If I had any in me) scholarship,
And from all learning keep these lines as clear
As Shakespeare's best are, which our heirs shall hear.

NOTE. From a recently discovered verse letter of the dramatist Beaumont to Ben Jonson. First printed by W. G. P. in *Times Literary Supplement,* Sept. 15, 1921, from an old commonplace book. The letter is signed F. B. and is not dated. It may be coeval with some well-known verses of Beaumont to Jonson, which are assigned to the period 1608-1610.

LV. BURIAL OF GILBERT SHAKESPEARE (1612).

Stratford Burial Register.

1611 [i.e. 1612]   *February 3   Gilbertus Shakspere, adolescens.*

NOTE. This was almost certainly the poet's brother, who had acted as his agent in the purchase of land from the Combes in 1602. (See no. XXXIV.) The identification has been doubted on the ground that the word *adolescens* is a strange one for a man of forty-five. A plausible explanation is offered by Mrs. Stopes, *Shakespeare's Environment,* pp. 332 ff.

LVI. SHAKESPEARE AS WITNESS IN THE BELOTT-MOUNTJOY SUIT (1612).

(Public Record Office, London.)

Stephen Belott, an apprentice of the French Huguenot tiremaker (wigmaker), Christopher Mountjoy, was married to his master's daughter, Mary Mountjoy, in St. Olave's Church, Silver St., London, November 19, 1604. On January 28, 1612, Belott brought suit in the court of requests against his father-in-law, alleging that Mountjoy had not fulfilled a promise to pay 'threescore pounds or thereabouts for a portion' at the time of the marriage and also to leave the couple two hundred pounds more on his decease. Shakespeare, who had been living in Mountjoy's house at the time and had taken part in the ante-matrimonial negotiations of Belott and Mountjoy, was cited as a witness in the case.

(A) Summons to Shakespeare and others, May 7, 1612.

Septimo die Maij. A compulsory to William Shakespeare gent. and others ad testificandum inter Stephanum Bellott querentem et Xpoferum [Christoferum] *Mountjoy defendentem.* r[eturnable] *Imed*[iately].

(B) List of witnesses examined:

| Stephen Belott
   plaintiff
Xpofer Mountjoy
   deft. | *Daniel Nicholas*
Johan(na) *Johnson uxor*
Tho. Johnson
William Shakespeare gent. |

(C) *Interrogatories to be ministered to witnesses to be produced on the part and behalf of Stephen Belott, Compl*[ainan]*t against Christopher Mountjoy, Def*[endan]*t.*

1. *Imprimis, whether do you know the parties pl*[ain]*t*[iff] *and deft. and how long have you known them and either of them?*

2. *Item, whether did you know the Complt. when he was servant with the said deft., how and in what sort did he behave himself in the service of the said deft., and whether did not the said deft. confess that he had got great profit and commodity by the service of the said Complt.?*

3. *Item, whether did not the said deft. seem to bear great good will and affection towards the said Complt. . . . and whether did not the said Deft. make a motion unto the said Complt. of marriage with the said Mary in the bill mentioned, being the said Deft's sole child and daughter . . . and whether did not he likewise send any person or no to persuade the said Complt. to the same? Declare the truth of your knowledge herein.*

4. *Item, what sum or sums of money did the said Deft. promise to give the said Complt. for a portion in marriage with the said Mary his daughter, whether the sum of threescore pounds, or what other sum as you know or have heard? . . .*

5. *Item, what parcels of goods or household stuff did the defendt promise to give unto the compl*[ainant] *in marriage with his said wife?* . . .

(D) The first witness examined, Joan Johnson, who had been a servant in Mountjoy's household, testified in answer to the third interrogatory *that the defendant seemed to bear great good will and affection towards the plaintiff . . . and as she remembereth the defendant did send and persuade one Mr. Shakespeare that lay in the house to persuade the plaintiff to the same marriage.*

(E) Daniel Nicholas, Gent., testified as follows:

To the third interrogatory this deponent saith he heard one Wm. Shakespeare say that the defendant did bear a good opinion of the plaintiff and affected him well when he served him; and did move the plaintiff by him the said Shakespeare to have a marriage between his daughter, Mary Montjoy, and the plaintiff; and for that purpose sent him, the said Shakespeare, to the plaintiff to persuade the plaintiff to the same, as Shakespeare told him, this deponent . . . To the fourth interrogatory this deponent saith that the plaintiff did request him, this deponent, to go with his wife to Shakespeare, to understand the truth, how much and what the defendant did promise to bestow on his daughter in marriage with him the plaintiff; who did so, and asking Shakespeare thereof, he answered that he promised, if the plaintiff would marry with Mary, his the defendant's only daughter, he the defendant would by his promise, as he remembered, give the plaintiff with her in marriage about the sum of fifty pounds in money and certain household stuff. . . .

(F) Shakespeare's deposition:[1]

William Shakespeare of Stratford-upon-Avon in the county of Warwick, gentleman, of the age of forty-eight years or thereabouts, sworn and examined the day and year abovesaid [i.e. May 11, 1612], *deposeth and saith:*

1. *To the first interrogatory this deponent saith he knoweth the parties plaintiff and defendant and hath known them both, as he now remembereth, for the space of ten years or thereabouts.*

2. *To the second interrogatory this deponent saith he did know the complainant when he was servant with the defendant, and that during the time of his the complainant's service with the said defendant he the said complainant to this deponent's knowledge did well and honestly behave himself, but to this deponent's remembrance he hath not heard the defendant confess that he had got any great profit and commodity by the service of the said complainant; but this deponent saith he verily thinketh that the said complainant was a very good and industrious servant in the said service. And more he cannot depose to the said interrogatory.*

3. *To the third interrogatory this deponent saith that it did evidently appear that the said defendant did all the time of the said complainant's service with him bear and show great good will and affection towards the said complainant, and that he hath heard the defendant and his wife divers and sundry times say and report that the said complainant was a very honest fellow. And this deponent saith that the said defendant did make a motion unto the complainant of*

---

1 See frontispiece for facsimile of this document. Abbreviated words have been expanded.

marriage with the said Mary in the bill mentioned, being the said defendant's sole child and daughter, and willingly offered to perform the same if the said complainant should seem to be content and well like thereof. And further this deponent saith that the said defendant's wife did solicit and entreat this deponent to move and persuade the said complainant to effect the said marriage; and accordingly this deponent did move and persuade the complainant thereunto. And more to this interrogatory he cannot depose.

4. To the fourth interrogatory this deponent saith that the defendant promised to give the said complainant a portion[1] in marriage with Mary his daughter; but what certain portion he remembereth not, nor when to be paid, nor knoweth that the defendant promised the plaintiff two hundred pounds with his daughter Mary at the time of his decease. But saith that the plaintiff was dwelling with the defendant in his house, and they had amongst themselves many conferences about their marriage, which . . .[2] was consummated and solemnized. .And more he cannot [depose.][2]

5. To the fifth interrogatory this deponent saith he can say noth[ing][2] touching any part or point of the same interrogatory, for he knoweth not what implements and necessaries of household stuff the defendant gave the plaintiff in marriage with his daughter Mary.

Willm Shakper[3]

This is Shakespeare's only deposition in the case. Other witnesses were later interrogated, several of

---

1 There are several cancelled passages in this part of the paper.
2 Paper torn.
3 This is the best extant signature of Shakespeare. The 'k,' however, has been spoiled by a blot of ink and the following 's' omitted. The crossed 'p' at the end was a conventional symbol for 'per.'

whom mention conversations they had had with Mr. Shakespeare. It appears from the evidence that Mountjoy's house, in which Shakespeare was living from about 1602, stood on the corner of Muggle (Monkwell) and Silver streets. The court finally adopted the strange expedient of referring the matter to the authorities of the French Church in London, who decided in favor of Belott and gave Mountjoy a very bad general moral character. The documents were discovered by Professor C. W. Wallace and printed by him *in extenso* in the *University Studies* of the University of Nebraska, 1910.

LVII. BURIAL OF RICHARD, THE POET'S BROTHER (1613).

Stratford Burial Register.

1612 [i.e. 1613] *February 4 Rich. Shakspeare.*

NOTE. Richard, whose burial occurred just a year and a day after that of Gilbert (see no. LV), appears to have been the last surviving brother of the poet.

LVIII. SHAKESPEARE PURCHASES A HOUSE IN BLACKFRIARS, LONDON (1613).

Deed from Henry Walker to Shakespeare and his Trustees, March 10, 1613.

This indenture, made the tenth day of March in the year of our Lord God, according to the computation of the Church of England, one thousand, six hundred and twelve [i.e. 1613] *. . . between Henry Walker, citizen and minstrel of London, of the one party, and William Shakespeare of Stratford-upon-Avon in the county of Warwick, gentleman, William Johnson, citizen and vintner of London, John Jackson, and John*

Hemmyng of London, gentlemen, of the other party,
Witnesseth that the said Henry Walker, for and in
consideration of the sum of one hundred and forty
pounds of lawful money of England to him in hand
before the ensealing hereof by the said William Shake-
speare well and truly paid . . ., hath bargained and
sold, and by these presents doth fully, clearly and
absolutely bargain and sell unto the said William
Shakespeare, William Johnson, John Jackson, and
John Hemmyng, their heirs and assigns for ever all
that dwelling-house or tenement, with the appurte-
nances, situate and being within the precinct, circuit,
and compass of the late Black Friars, London, some-
times [i.e. formerly] in the tenure of James Gardyner,
Esq., and since that in the tenure of John Fortescue,
Gent., and now or late being in the tenure or occupa-
tion of one William Ireland, or of his assignee or
assigns, abutting upon a street leading down to Puddle
Wharf on the east part, right against the King's Maj-
esty's Wardrobe; part of which said tenement is
erected over a great gate leading to a capital messuage
which sometime was in the tenure of William Black-
well, Esq., deceased, and since that in the tenure or
occupation of the Right Honorable Henry, now Earl
of Northumberland; and also all that plot of ground
on the west side of the said tenement, which was lately
enclosed with boards on two sides thereof by Anne
Bacon, widow . . . which said dwelling-house or tene-
ment, and other the premises above by these presents
mentioned to be bargained and sold, the said Henry
Walker late purchased and had to him, his heirs and
assigns for ever, of Mathie Bacon, of Gray's Inn in
the county of Midd., gentleman, by indenture bearing
date the fifteenth day of October, in the year of our

*Lord God one thousand, six hundred and four . . .
And further that all and every fine and fines to be
levied, recoveries to be suffered, estates and assur-
ances at any time or times hereafter to be had, made,
executed or passed by or between the said parties of
the premises, or of any parcel thereof, shall be, and
shall be esteemed, adjudged, deemed and taken to be
to the only and proper use and behoof of the said
William Shakespeare, his heirs and assigns, for ever,
and to none other use, intent or purpose. . . .*

NOTE. There are two copies of this deed. One, signed
by Shakespeare and two of his trustees (Johnson and
Jackson) and intended to be retained by the vendor,
is in the Guildhall, London. The other, signed by
Walker, and delivered to Shakespeare, was formerly
in the possession of Halliwell-Phillipps, and now be-
longs to Mr. H. C. Folger. The document makes it
clear that the property was purchased by Shakespeare
and that Johnson, Jackson, and Hemming were merely
acting as trustees in his interest. Whether the John
Hemming who figures here is identical with the actor-
friend of the poet is uncertain.

Sir Sidney Lee conjectures that the employment of
the trustees was a legal device adopted in order to
defeat Shakespeare's widow's claim to dower.

LIX. MORTGAGE DEED ON THE BLACK-FRIARS PROPERTY (1613).

British Museum, London.

In purchasing the property transferred to him and
his trustees by the deed of March 10, 1613, Shakespeare seems to have paid down £80 of the agreed
price of £140. On the following day he and his three

trustees gave the vendor, Henry Walker, a mortgage for the remaining sixty pounds. The terms of this document are that Walker is to regain possession of the Blackfriars property for a term of one hundred years from the feast of the annunciation next coming (March 25, 1613): *Provided always that if the said William Shakespeare, his heirs, executors, administrators or assigns, or any of them, do well and truly pay or cause to be paid to the said Henry Walker, his executors, administrators, or assigns, the sum of threescore pounds of lawful money of England in and upon the nine-and-twentieth day of September next coming after the date hereof, at or in the now dwelling-house of the said Henry Walker, situate and being in the parish of Saint Martin near Ludgate, of London, at one entire payment, without delay, that then and thenceforth this present lease, demise, and grant . . . shall cease, determine, and be utterly void, frustrate, and of none effect.*

NOTE. There is no evidence that this mortgage was paid off, except the fact that the property remained in Shakespeare's possession and was bequeathed in his will. On February 10, 1618, the poet's trustees, John Jackson, John Heminge, and William Johnson executed a document (Halliwell-Phillipps, *Outlines,* 7th ed., ii. 36-41) putting into effect the provision the poet's will made with reference to his Blackfriars property. (See p. 85.)

LX. SHAKESPEARE AND BURBAGE EMPLOYED BY THE EARL OF RUTLAND (1613).

From the Accounts of the Steward of the Earl of Rutland, Belvoir Castle Manuscripts.

1613 31 Martii. To Mr. Shakspeare in gold, about my Lord's impreso, xliv s. To Richard Burbage for painting and making it, in gold, xliv s. . . . iiii li. viii s.

NOTE. The *impresa,* or personal badge, was devised for a tilting match in which the Earl of Rutland took part, March 24, 1613. It doubtless took the form of a mythological or allegorical emblem of some sort. Burbage the actor was also a painter, and the mention of his name renders it probable that the Mr. Shakespeare associated with him was the poet. This document was discovered in 1907. For discussion of its authenticity see Mrs. Stopes, *Shakespeare's Environment,* p. 231.

LXI. THOMAS FREEMAN'S SONNET TO SHAKESPEARE (1614).

From *Run, and a Great Cast,* 2d part, 1614.

To Master W. Shakespeare.

Shakespeare, that nimble Mercury, thy brain,
Lulls many hundred Argus-eyes asleep,
So fit for all thou fashionest thy vein.
  At the horse-foot fountain[1] thou hast drunk full
      deep:
Virtue's or vice's theme to thee all one is.
  Who loves chaste life, there's Lucrece for a teacher;
Who list read lust, there's Venus and Adonis,
  True model of a most lascivious lecher.
Besides in plays thy wit winds like Meander,
  Whence needy new-composers borrow more

---

1 I.e. Hippocrene.

Than Terence doth from Plautus and Menander.
  But to praise thee aright I want thy store.
    Then let thine own works thine own worth up-
      raise,
    And help t'adorn thee with deserved bays.

LXII. BEQUEST TO SHAKESPEARE IN JOHN COMBE'S WILL (1614).

To Mr. William Shakespeare five pounds.

NOTE. John Combe, the wealthy bachelor with whom Shakespeare had had many business dealings, died in July, 1614. He was buried, like the poet, in the chancel of Stratford Church.

LXIII. AGREEMENT PROTECTING SHAKE- SPEARE AGAINST LOSS OF TITHE IN- COME BY REASON OF ENCLOSURES AT WELCOMBE (1614).

Contract of William Replingham, legal agent for the Combes, with Shakespeare and his cousin, Thomas Greene, October 28, 1614.

Vicesimo octavo die Octobris, anno Domini 1614. Articles of agreement indented [and] made between Willm. Shackespeare of Stretford in the county of War- wick, gent., on the one party and Willm. Replingham of Great Harborowe in the county of Warwick, gent., on the other party, the day and year abovesaid. Item, the said Willm. Replingham for him, his heirs, execu- tors, and assigns, doth covenant and agree to and with the said Willm. Shackespeare, his heirs and assigns, that he, the said Willm. Replingham, his heirs or assigns, shall upon reasonable request satisfy, content, and make recompense unto him the said Willm. Shackespeare or his assigns for all such loss, detriment, and hinderance as he, the said Willm. Shackespeare, his heirs and assigns, and one Thomas Greene, gent., shall or may be thought in the view and judgment of four indifferent persons, to be indifferently elected by the said Willm. and Willm. and their heirs, and in default of the said Willm. Replingham by the said Willm. Shackespeare or his heirs only, to survey and judge the same to sustain or incur for or in respect of the increasing[1] of the yearly value of the tithes they, the said Willm. Shackespeare and Thomas, do jointly or severally hold and enjoy in the said fields or any of them by reason of any inclosure or decay of tillage there meant and intended by the said Willm. Replingham; and that the said Willm. Replingham and his heirs shall procure such sufficient security unto the said Willm. Shackespeare and his heirs for the performance of these covenants as shall be devised by learned counsel. In witness whereof the parties abovesaid to these presents interchangeably their hands and seals have put the day and year first above written.

NOTE. A facsimile of this document is given by Halliwell-Phillipps, *Outlines,* 7th ed., ii. 38, 39. The object of the agreement was to prevent Shakespeare's personal opposition to William Combe's project of enclosing and appropriating the 'common fields' of Welcombe. Shakespeare and his cousin, Greene, both had tithe rights in this neighborhood which would be affected by the enclosures. See the next document.

---

1 So the manuscript: perhaps a slip for 'decreasing.'

LXIV. NOTES OF THOMAS GREENE CONCERNING SHAKESPEARE'S ATTITUDE TOWARD THE PROPOSED ENCLOSURES AT WELCOMBE (1614-1615).

MS. notes by Greene, Town Clerk of Stratford, Shakespeare's cousin and attorney. (Shakespeare Birthplace Museum.)

(A) *5 Septembris, 1614.*
Ancient Freeholders in the Fields of Old Stratford and Welcombe. Mr. Shakspeare: 4 yard land.[1] *No common nor ground beyond Gospel Bush; no ground in Sandfield, nor none in Slow Hill Field beyond Bishopton, nor none in the enclosure beyond Bishopton.*

(B) *Jovis* [Thursday] *17 Nov.* [1614]. *My cousin Shakspeare coming* [?] *yesterday to town, I went to see him how he did.*[2] *He told me that they assured him they meant to enclose no further than to Gospel Bush, and so up straight (leaving out part of the dingles to the field) to the gate in Clopton hedge, and take in Salisbury's piece* [?]; *and that they mean in April to survey the land, and then to give satisfaction and not before; and he and Mr. Hall say they think there will be nothing done at all.*

(C) *23 Dec.* [1614]. *A Hall.*[3] *Letters written, one to Mr. Mannering, another to Mr. Shakspeare, with almost all the company's hands to either. I also writ of myself to my Cousin Shakspear the copies of all our acts, and then also a note of the inconveniences would grow* [?] *by the enclosure.*[4]

---

1 This is the land bought by Shakespeare from the Combes. See documents XXXIV and LII.
2 Greene was in London at this time, but returned to Stratford before the date of the next note (Dec. 23), Shakespeare evidently remaining in the city.
3 I.e. meeting of the Stratford town council.
4 The letter of the Stratford corporation to Mannering, pro-

(D) *9 Jan.* [1615]. *Mr. Replingham, 28 Octobris, articled with Mr. Shakspear, and then I was put in by T. Lucas.*[1]

(E) *On Wednesday, being the 11th day* [of January, 1615]. *At night Mr. Replingham supped with me, and Mr. W. Barnes was to bear him company, where he assured me before Mr. Barnes that I should be well dealt withal, confessing former promises by himself, Mr. Mannering, and his agreement for me with my Cousin Shakspeare.*

(F) *Sept.* [1615]. *W. Shakespeare's telling J. Greene that I*[2] *was not able to bear the enclosing of Welcombe.*

NOTE. Combe's high-handed effort to appropriate common property led to violent opposition from the burghers of Stratford. The quarrel was carried to the Privy Council of England and finally resulted, a couple of years after Shakespeare's death, in the discomfiture of Combe and the overthrow of the projects for enclosure. The best account of the affair is that of Mrs. Stopes, *Shakespeare's Environment*, pp. 81 ff. and 336 ff.

LXV. FRIENDLY CHANCERY SUIT OF SHAKESPEARE AND OTHERS CONCERNING DOCUMENTS RELATING TO HIS PROPERTY IN BLACKFRIARS (1615).

(A) Petition of Shakespeare and other owners of property in Blackfriars to compel Matthew Bacon to

testing against enclosures, is preserved (cf. Mrs. Stopes, *Shakespeare's Environment*, p. 337). The two letters to Shakespeare are lost.

[1] This alludes, of course, to Shakespeare's agreement with Replingham (see previous document). T. Lucas was one of the witnesses to it.

[2] This may be a slip of the pen for 'he' (Shakespeare).

produce the old papers necessary to the establishment
of their respective titles. (Public Record Office, London.)

*xxvj*to *die Aprilis, 1615. To the Right Honorable
Sir Thomas Egerton, Knight, Lord Ellesmere and
Lord Chancellor of England. Humbly complaining
showeth unto your honorable Lordship your daily
orators, Sir Thomas Bendish, Baronet, Edward Newport and William Thoresbie, Esq., Robert Dormer,
Esq., and Mary his wife, William Shakespere, Gent.,
and Richard Bacon, citizen of London, that whereas
your orators be and are severally lawfully seised in
their demesne as of fee* [in various specified pieces of
real estate] . . . *all which messuages, tenements, and
premises aforesaid be lying within the precinct of
Blackfriars in the city of London. . . . Unto which
foresaid capital messuages, tenements, and premises
aforesaid several deeds, charters, letters patents, evidences, muniments, and writings be and are belonging
and appertaining, and do belong unto your orators,
and do serve for the proving of your orators' lawful
right, title, interest, and estate into and unto the foresaid messuages and premises: all which foresaid letters
patents, deeds, evidences, charters, muniments, and
writings aforesaid were left in trust with Ann Bacon,
deceased, for and unto the use and behoof of your
orators. . . .*

The document proceeds to declare that on Ann
Bacon's death the papers in question passed into the
possession of Matthew Bacon, her sole executor, and
begs that the said Matthew be required to *appear before your Lordship in his Majesty's high court of
chancery, then and there for to make answer unto the*

*premisses and also to bring with him the said letters
patents, deeds, evidences, charters, and writings into
this honorable court and to stand to and abide such
further orders therein as to your honorable Lordship
shall be thought fit. . . .*

(B) *5 Maij, 1615. The answer of Mathy Bacon,
gent., defendant, to the bill of complaint of Sir
Thomas Bendish, Baronet, Edward Newport, Esq.,
William Thoresby, Esq., Robert Dormer, Esq., and
Mary his wife, William Shakespeare, gent., and Rich-
ard Bacon, citizen of London, complainants.*

Matthew Bacon answers that he thinks the statements of the complainants to be true, and that he does
not himself claim any title to their respective proper-
ties, but that he does not certainly know whether the
documents demanded belong exclusively to the complainants or whether other persons may have a claim
to them. Provided he may be relieved of all future
responsibility regarding the papers in his possession,
he is ready to deliver them to such person or persons
and in such sort as the court shall order.

(C) The court's decree. *xxij die Maii.* After
briefly recapitulating the statements in the two preceding papers, *It is thereupon ordered that the said
defendant shall bring into this court all the said letters
patents, deeds, evidences, writings, and muniments so
by him confessed to be in his custody or possession
upon his oath, here to remain to be disposed of as shall
be meet, and for that purpose the plaintiffs may take
process against the defendant if they will.*

NOTE. These papers were discovered by Professor
C. W. Wallace, and printed in *University Studies* of

the University of Nebraska, 1905, with a commentary
which inaccurately represents the attitude of the
parties to the suit. There was no quarrel, but Matthew
Bacon, as executor for his mother's estate, required
authorization of the court before surrendering the
documents. As stated in Shakespeare's deed for his
Blackfriars property (see p. 71), Henry Walker, who
sold it to the poet, had himself bought it in 1604 from
'Mathie' Bacon (the father).[1] The difficulty about the
deeds arose from the intricate way in which the valu-
able and fashionable residence property at Blackfriars
had been subdivided. Sections covered by a single
early deed or charter were in Shakespeare's day held
by many owners, all of whom would require to have
access to the old papers in tracing their titles.

The names of most of the complainants associated
with Shakespeare indicate the high social standing of
his neighbors in the Blackfriars district.

LXVI. MARRIAGE OF SHAKESPEARE'S YOUNGER DAUGHTER (1616).

Stratford Marriage Register.

1615 [i.e. 1616] *February 10   Tho. Queeny to
Judith Shakspere.*

NOTE. Thomas Quyny, son of Shakespeare's friend,
Richard Quyny, was baptized February 26, 1589, being four years younger than Judith Shakespeare. He
was a vintner or inn-keeper by trade and apparently
a shiftless person.

1 Mathias Bacon of Holborn, London, was a scrivener, admitted
to Gray's Inn, March 1, 1597 (Joseph Foster, *Register of Admissions
to Gray's Inn*, p. 91; Basil Brown, *Law Sports at Gray's Inn*, p. 29).
This was probably Anne Bacon's husband.

LXVII. SHAKESPEARE'S WILL (1616).

(Preserved in Somerset House, London.)

Vicesimo quinto die Martii anno regni domini nostri Jacobi nunc Regis Anglie &c. decimo quarto & Scotie xlix° Annoque Domini 1616.[1]

T. Wmi. Shackspeare.[2]

In the name of God, Amen. I, William Shackspeare of Stratford-upon-Avon in the county of Warwick, gent., in perfect health and memory, God be praised, do make and ordain this my last will and testament in manner and form following. That is to say: First I commend my soul into the hands of God my Creator, hoping and assuredly believing through the only merits of Jesus Christ my Saviour to be made partaker of life everlasting; and my body to the earth whereof it is made.

Item, I give and bequeath unto my daughter Judith one hundred and fifty pounds of lawful English money to be paid unto her in manner and form following, that is to say: one hundred pounds [in discharge of her marriage portion][3] within one year after my decease with consideration after the rate of two shillings in the pound for so long time as the same shall be unpaid unto her after my decease, and the fifty pounds' residue thereof upon her surrendering [of] or giving of such sufficient security as the overseers of this my will shall like of to surrender or grant all her estate and right that shall descend or come unto her after my

---

1 'On the 25th day of March in the year of the reign of our lord James, now King of England, etc., the fourteenth, and of Scotland the forty-ninth, and in the year of our Lord, 1616.' The month was originally given as *Januarij*, for which March was later substituted.

2 'T[estamentum] of William Shackspeare.'

3 The bracketed words, here and later, are written in above the lines.

decease or [that she] now hath of, in, or to one copy-
hold tenement[1] with the appurtenances, lying and be-
ing in Stratford-upon-Avon aforesaid in the said county
of Warwick, being parcel or holden of the manor of
Rowington, unto my daughter Susanna Hall and her
heirs forever. Item, I give and bequeath unto my said
daughter Judith one hundred and fifty pounds more,
if she or any issue of her body be living at the end of
three years next ensuing the day of the date of this my
will, during which time my executors to pay her con-
sideration from my decease according to the rate afore-
said. And if she die within the said term without issue
of her body, then my will is and I do give and be-
queath one hundred pounds thereof to my niece,[2]
Elizabeth Hall, and the fifty pounds to be set forth by
my executors during the life of my sister, Joan Hart,
and the use and profit thereof coming shall be paid to
my said sister Joan, and after her decease the said
fifty pounds shall remain amongst the children of my
said sister, equally to be divided amongst them. But
if my said daughter Judith be living at the end of the
said three years, or any issue of her body, then my will
is and so I devise and bequeath the said hundred and
fifty pounds to be set out [by my executors and over-
seers] for the best benefit of her and her issue, and
[the stock] not [to be] paid unto her so long as she
shall be married and covert baron; but my will is that
she shall have the consideration yearly paid unto her
during her life and after her decease the said stock
and consideration to be paid to her children if she have
any, and if not to her executors or assigns, she living
the said term after my decease. Provided that if such
husband as she shall at the end of the said three years

1 For the property here referred to see document XXXVI.
2 That is, granddaughter, as commonly in Shakespeare's plays.

*be married unto or attain after do sufficiently assure
unto her and the issue of her body lands answerable
to the portion by this my will given unto her and to
be adjudged so by my executors and overseers, then
my will is that the said 150 pounds shall be paid to
such husband as shall make such assurance, to his own
use.*

*Item, I give and bequeath unto my said sister Joan
20 pounds and all my wearing apparel, to be paid and
delivered within one year after my decease, and I do
will and devise unto her [the house] with the appurtenances in Stratford wherein she dwelleth for her
natural life under the yearly rent of twelvepence.
Item, I give and bequeath unto her three sons, William
Hart, —— Hart,[1] and Michael Hart, five pounds
apiece, to be paid within one year after my decease.*

*Item, I give and bequeath unto [the said Elizabeth
Hall] all my plate [except my broad silver and gilt
bowl] that I now have at the date of this my will.
Item, I give and bequeath unto the poor of Stratford
aforesaid ten pounds; to Mr. Thomas Combe my
sword; to Thomas Russell, Esq., five pounds; and to
Francis Collins[2] of the borough of Warwick in the
county of Warwick, gent., thirteen pounds, six shillings, and eightpence, to be paid within one year after
my decease. Item, I give and bequeath to Hamlet
Sadler 26 s. 8 d. to buy him a ring; [to William Rey-
nolds, gent., 26 s. 8 d. to buy him a ring]; to my godson, William Walker, 20 s. in gold; to Anthony Nashe,
gent., 26 s. 8 d. and to Mr. John Nashe 26 s. 8 d.,*

---

[1] The nephew whose name had slipped Shakespeare's memory
was Thomas Hart. He was ten years old at the time and lived till
1661, long surviving his brothers and leaving a line of posterity still
extant.

[2] Francis Collins was the lawyer in whose handwriting the will
is written.

[*and to my fellows, John Hemings, Richard Burbage, and Henry Condell 26 s. 8 d apiece to buy them rings*].

Item *I give, will, bequeath, and devise unto my daughter Susanna Hall* [*for better enabling of her to perform this my will and towards the performance thereof*] *all that capital messuage or tenement with the appurtenances* [*in Stratford aforesaid*] *called the New Place,*[1] *wherein I now dwell, and two messuages or tenements*[2] *with the appurtenances situate, lying, and being in Henley Street within the borough of Stratford aforesaid; and all my barns, stables, orchards, gardens, lands, tenements, and hereditaments whatsoever, situate, lying and being, or to be had, received, perceived or taken, within the towns, hamlets, villages, fields, and grounds of Stratford-upon-Avon, Old Stratford, Bushopton, and Welcombe,*[3] *or in any of them, in the said county of Warwick; and also all that messuage or tenement with the appurtenances wherein one John Robinson dwelleth,*[4] *situate, lying, and being in the Blackfriars in London, near the Wardrobe; and all other my lands, tenements, and hereditaments whatsoever, to have and to hold all and singular the said premises with their appurtenances unto the said Susanna Hall for and during the term of her natural life, and after her decease to the first son of her body lawfully issuing and to the heirs males of the body of the said first son lawfully issuing, and for default of such issue to the second son of her body lawfully issuing and to the heirs males of the body of the said second son lawfully issuing, and for default of such heirs to the third son of the body of the said*

1 Cf. document XV.
2 The birth-house property. Cf. document XXXI, Note.
3 Property covered by documents XXXIV, XLIV, LI, LII, LXIII, LXIV.
4 Property covered by documents LVIII, LIX, LXV. Shakespeare had rented the Blackfriars house to John Robinson.

*Susanna lawfully issuing and of the heirs males of the
body of the said third son lawfully issuing; and for
default of such issue the same so to be and remain to the
fourth, fifth, sixth, and seventh sons of her body lawfully issuing, one after another, and to the heirs males
of the bodies of the said fourth, fifth, sixth, and seventh
sons lawfully issuing in such manner as it is before
limited, to be and remain to the first, second, and
third sons of her body and to their heirs males. And
for default of such issue the said premises to be and
remain to my said niece Hall and the heirs males of
her body lawfully issuing; and for default of such
issue, to my daughter Judith and the heirs males of
her body lawfully issuing; and for default of such
issue to the right heirs of me the said William Shakspeare for ever. [Item, I give unto my wife my second
best bed with the furniture.] Item, I give and bequeath to my said daughter Judith my broad silver
gilt bowl. All the rest of my goods, chattel, leases,
plate, jewels and household stuff whatsoever after my
debts and legacies paid and my funeral expenses discharged I give, devise, and bequeath to my son-in-law,
John Hall, gent., and my daughter Susanna his wife,
whom I ordain and make executors of this my last will
and testament. And I do entreat and appoint [the
said] Thomas Russell, Esq., and Francis Collins,
gent., to be overseers hereof, and do revoke all former
wills and publish this to be my last will and testament.
In witness whereof I have hereunto put my hand the
day and year first above written.*

By me   William Shakspeare

NOTE. Shakespeare's will contains three signatures
of the poet, one at the bottom of each of the three

pages on which it is written. It was witnessed by Francis Collins, Julius Shaw, John Robinson, Hamnet Sadler, and Robert Whatcott, and was proved June 22, 1616.

LXVIII. SHAKESPEARE'S DEATH AND BURIAL (1616).

Stratford Burial Register.

1616   April 25   Will. Shakspere, gent.

NOTE. The date of Shakespeare's death, April 23, is indicated by the inscription on his monument in the chancel of Holy Trinity Church, Stratford:

*Judicio Pylium, genio Socratem, arte Maronem
Terra tegit, populus moeret, Olympus habet.*

*Stay, passenger, why goest thou by so fast?
Read, if thou canst, whom envious death hath placed
Within this monument: Shakespeare, with whom
Quick nature died; whose name doth deck his tomb
Far more than cost; sith all that he hath writ
Leaves living art but page to serve his wit.*

Obiit an[n]*o do*[min]*i 1616. Ætatis 53.   Die 23 Ap.*

Shakespeare's brother-in-law, William Hart, husband of his sister Joan (who survived till 1646), was buried in the same church on April 17, during the previous week.

LXIX. INTRODUCTORY MATTER TO THE SHAKESPEARE FOLIO (1623).

(A) Dedicatory Epistle of Heminge and Condell to the Earls of Pembroke and Montgomery.

To the most noble and incomparable pair of breth-ren: William, Earl of Pembroke, &c., Lord Chamber-lain to the King's most excellent Majesty; and Philip, Earl of Montgomery, &c., Gentleman of his Majesty's Bedchamber—both Knights of the most noble Order of the Garter, and our singular good lords.

Right Honorable:

Whilst we study to be thankful in our particular for the many favors we have received from your Lord-ships, we are fallen upon the ill fortune to mingle two the most diverse things that can be: fear and rash-ness—rashness in the enterprise, and fear of the suc-cess. For when we value the places your Highnesses sustain, we cannot but know their dignity greater than to descend to the reading of these trifles; and while we name them trifles, we have deprived ourselves of the defence of our dedication.

But since your Lordships have been pleased to think these trifles something heretofore, and have prosecuted both them and their author, living, with so much favor, we hope that (they outliving him, and he not having the fate, common with some, to be executor to his own writings) you will use the like indulgence toward them you have done unto their parent. There is a great difference whether any book choose his patrons or find them. This hath done both. For so much were your Lordships' likings of the several parts, when they were acted, as before they were published the volume asked to be yours. We have but collected them, and done an office to the dead, to procure his orphans guardians: without ambition either of self-profit or fame, only to keep the memory of so worthy a friend and fellow alive as was our SHAKESPEARE by humble offer of his plays to your most noble patron-

*age.   Wherein, as we have justly observed no man to
come near your Lordships but with a kind of religious
address, it hath been the height of our care, who are
the presenters, to make the present worthy of your
Highnesses by the perfection.*

*But there we must also crave our abilities to be con-
sidered, my Lords.   We cannot go beyond our own
powers: country hands reach forth milk, cream, fruits,
or what they have; and many nations, we have heard,
that had not gums and incense, obtained their requests
with a leavened cake.   It was no fault to approach their
gods by what means they could; and the most, though
meanest, of things are made more precious when they
are dedicated to temples.   In that name, therefore, we
most humbly consecrate to your Highnesses these remains of your servant* Shakespeare: *that what delight
is in them may be ever your Lordships', the reputation
his, and the faults ours, if any be committed by a pair
so careful to show their gratitude both to the living
and the dead as is*

Your Lordships' most bounden

JOHN HEMINGE

HENRY CONDELL

(B) Epistle of Heminge and Condell to the **readers**
of the Folio.

*To the Great Variety of Readers.—From the most
able to him that can but spell: there you are num-
bered.   We had rather you were weighed; especially
when the fate of all books depends upon your capacities, and not of your heads alone, but of your purses.
Well, it is now public, and you will stand for your
privileges, we know: to read and censure.   Do so, but
buy it first: that doth best commend a book, the sta-*

tioner says. Then, how odd soever your brains be or your wisdoms, make your license the same, and spare not. Judge your six-penn'orth, your shilling's worth, your five shillings' worth at a time, or higher, so you rise to the just rates, and welcome. But, whatever you do, buy! Censure will not drive a trade or make the jack go. And though you be a magistrate of wit, and sit on the stage at Blackfriars or the Cockpit to arraign plays daily, know, these plays have had their trial already and stood out all appeals, and do now come forth quitted rather by a decree of court than any purchased letters of commendation.

It had been a thing, we confess, worthy to have been wished that the author himself had lived to have set forth and overseen his own writings; but since it hath been ordained otherwise, and he by death departed from that right, we pray you, do not envy his friends the office of their care and pain, to have collected and published them:—and so to have published them, as where before you were abused with divers stolen and surreptitious copies, maimed and deformed by the frauds and stealths of injurious impostors that exposed them, even those are now offered to your view cured and perfect of their limbs, and all the rest absolute in their numbers as he conceived them,—who, as he was a happy imitator of nature, was a most gentle expresser of it. His mind and hand went together, and what he thought he uttered with that easiness that we have scarce received from him a blot in his papers. But it is not our province, who only gather his works and give them you, to praise him: it is yours' that read him. And there, we hope, to your divers capacities, you will find enough both to draw and hold you; for his wit can no more lie hid than it

*could be lost. Read him, therefore, and again and
again; and if then you do not like him, surely you are
in some manifest danger not to understand him, and
so we leave you to other of his friends whom if you
need can be your guides. If you need them not, you
can lead yourselves and others, and such readers we
wish him.*

John Heminge.
Henry Condell.

(C) Ben Jonson's Eulogy.

To the memory of my beloved, the Author, Mr.
WILLIAM SHAKESPEARE, *and what he hath left us.*

To draw no envy, Shakespeare, on thy name,
Am I thus ample to thy book and fame,
While I confess thy writings to be such
As neither man nor muse can praise too much.
'Tis true, and all men's suffrage. But these ways
Were not the paths I meant unto thy praise:
For silliest ignorance on these may light,
Which, when it sounds at best, but echoes right;
Or blind affection, which doth ne'er advance
The truth, but gropes, and urgeth all by chance;
Or crafty malice might pretend this praise,
And think to ruin where it seem'd to raise.
These are as some infamous bawd or whore
Should praise a matron: what could hurt her more?
But thou art proof against them, and indeed
Above th' ill fortune of them, or the need.

I therefore will begin:—Soul of the age!
The applause, delight, the wonder of our stage!
My Shakespeare, rise! I will not lodge thee by
Chaucer or Spenser, or bid Beaumont lie

A little further, to make thee a room.[1]
Thou art a monument without a tomb,
And art alive still, while thy book doth live
And we have wits to read and praise to give.
That I not mix thee so[2] *my brain excuses—*
I mean with great but disproportion'd muses—
For if I thought my judgment were of years,[3]
I should commit thee surely with thy peers,
And tell how far thou didst our Lyly outshine,
Or sporting Kyd, or Marlowe's mighty line.
And though thou hadst small Latin and less Greek,
From thence to honor thee I would not seek
For names, but call forth thund'ring Æschylus,
Euripides, and Sophocles to us,
Pacuvius, Accius, him of Cordova,[4] *dead*
To life again, to hear thy buskin tread
And shake a stage: or, when thy socks[5] *were on,*
Leave thee alone for the comparison
Of all that insolent Greece or haughty Rome
Sent forth, or since did from their ashes come.

Triumph, my Britain! Thou hast one to show,
To whom all scenes of Europe homage owe.
He was not of an age, but for all time;
And all the muses still were in their prime
When, like Apollo, he came forth to warm
Our ears, or like a Mercury to charm.
Nature herself was proud of his designs,
And joyed to wear the dressing of his lines,
Which were so richly spun and woven so fit
As, since, she will vouchsafe no other wit.

1 Beaumont had been buried, a few months before Shakespeare's death, in Westminster Abbey, where Chaucer and Spenser also lay.
2 I.e. with Chaucer, Spenser, and Beaumont.
3 I.e. mature.
4 Seneca, born at Cordova.
5 Comedies.

The merry Greek, tart Aristophanes,
Neat Terence, witty Plautus, now not please,
But antiquated and deserted lie
As they were not of nature's family.

Yet must I not give nature all: thy art,
My gentle Shakespeare, must enjoy a part;
For though the poet's matter nature be,
His art doth give the fashion; and that he,
Who casts to write a living line, must sweat
(Such as thine are), and strike the second heat
Upon the muses' anvil—turn the same
(And himself with it) that he thinks to frame,
Or for the laurel he may gain a scorn:
For a good poet's made as well as born,
And such wert thou.   Look, how the father's face
Lives in his issue, even so the race
Of Shakespeare's mind and manners brightly shines
In his well-turned and true-filed lines,
In each of which he seems to shake a lance,
As brandish'd at the eyes of ignorance.

Sweet swan of Avon! what a sight it were
To see thee in our waters yet appear,
And make those flights upon the banks of Thames
That so did take Eliza and our James!
But stay, I see thee in the hemisphere
Advanc'd and made a constellation there.
Shine forth, thou star of poets, and with rage,
Or influence, chide or cheer the drooping stage,
Which since thy flight fro hence hath mourn'd like
*   night,*
And despairs day but for thy volume's light.

BEN: JONSON.

(D) Elegiac sonnet of Hugh Holland.

Upon the Lines and Life of the Famous Scenic Poet,
Master WILLIAM SHAKESPEARE.

Those hands which you so clapp'd, go now and wring,
    You Britons brave, for done are Shakespeare's days:
    His days are done that made the dainty plays,
Which made the Globe of heaven and earth to ring.
Dried is that vein, dried is the Thespian spring,
    Turn'd all to tears, and Phoebus clouds his rays:
    That corpse, that coffin, now bestick those bays
Which crown'd him poet first, then poets' king.

If tragedies might any prologue have,
    All those he made would scarce make one to this,
Where Fame, now that he gone is to the grave,
    Death's public tiring-house, the Nuncius[1] *is:*
        For though his line of life went soon about,
        The life yet of his lines shall never out.

                                    HUGH HOLLAND

(E) Dedicatory verses by Leonard Digges.

To the Memory of the deceased Author, Master W.
SHAKESPEARE.

Shake-speare, at length thy pious fellows give
The world thy works: thy works, by which outlive
Thy tomb thy name must. When that stone is rent,
And time dissolves thy Stratford monument,
Here we alive shall view thee still: this book,
When brass and marble fade, shall make thee look
Fresh to all ages. When posterity
Shall loath what's new, think all is prodigy

1 The messenger in Senecan tragedy who reported the deaths to
the audience.

That is not Shake-speare's every line, each verse
Here shall revive, redeem thee from thy hearse.
Nor fire nor cankering age, as Naso said
Of his, thy wit-fraught book shall once invade.
Nor shall I e'er believe or think thee dead
(Though miss'd), until our bankrout[1] stage be sped
(Impossible!) with some new strain t' outdo
Passions of Juliet and her Romeo;
Or till I hear a scene more nobly take
Than when thy half-sword-parleying[2] Romans spake.
Till these, till any of thy volume's rest,
Shall with more fire, more feeling, be express'd,
Be sure, our Shake-speare, thou canst never die,
But, crown'd with laurel, live eternally.

L. DIGGES[3]

(F) Memorial Verses by James Mabbe.

To the memory of M. W. Shake-speare.

We wondered, Shake-speare, that thou went'st so soon
From the world's stage to the grave's tiring-room.
We thought thee dead, but this thy printed worth
Tells thy spectators that thou went'st but forth
To enter with applause. An actor's art
Can die, and live to act a second part:
That's[4] but an exit of mortality,
This[5] a re-entrance to a plaudite.[6]

I. M.

(G) List of the Principal Actors in Shakespeare's Plays.

---

1 Bankrupt.
2 I.e. Brutus and Cassius, parleying with swords half drawn.
3 A longer poem by Digges, in the same strain but with more detail, was printed in the 1640 edition of Shakespeare's *Poems.*
4 Shakespeare's death.
5 The appearance of the Folio.
6 The play's successful close.

The Names of the Principal Actors in all these plays.

William Shakespeare.	Samuel Gilburne.
Richard Burbadge.	Robert Armin.
John Hemmings.	William Ostler.
Augustine Phillips.	Nathan Field.
William Kempt.	John Underwood.
Thomas Poope.	Nicholas Tooley.
George Bryan.	William Ecclestone.
Henry Condell.	Joseph Taylor.
William Slye.	Robert Benfield.
Richard Cowly.	Robert Goughe.
John Lowine.	Richard Robinson.
Samuell Crosse.	John Shancke.
Alexander Cooke.	John Rice.

LXX. BEN JONSON ON SHAKESPEARE (1630?).

Section entitled *De Shakespeare nostrat[e]*[1] in Jonson's *Timber, or Discoveries,* printed posthumously, 1641.

I remember, the players have often mentioned it as an honor to Shakespeare that in his writing, whatsoever he penned, he never blotted out line.[2] *My answer hath been: Would he had blotted a thousand; which they thought a malevolent speech. I had not told posterity this but for their ignorance, who choose that circumstance to commend their friend by wherein he most faulted, and to justify mine own candor, for I loved the man and do honor his memory (on this side idolatry) as much as any. He was, indeed, honest, and of an open and free nature; had an excellent*

1 'Concerning Shakespeare, our countryman.'
2 Cf. Heminge and Condell, p. 90.

fancy, brave notions, and gentle expressions, wherein he flowed with that facility that sometime it was necessary he should be stopped: Sufflaminandus erat,[1] *as Augustus said of Haterius. His wit was in his own power; would the rule of it had been so too. Many times he fell into those things could not escape laughter: as when he said in the person of Cæsar, one speaking to him 'Cæsar, thou dost me wrong!'—he replied, 'Cæsar did never wrong but with just cause';*[2] *and such like, which were ridiculous. But he redeemed his vices with his virtues: there was ever more in him to be praised than to be pardoned.*

1 'He had to be checked.'
2 The passage in Jonson's mind is *Julius Cæsar* III. i. 47, which does not now stand as Jonson quotes it. The absence of precise logical consistency, which Jonson ascribes to too hasty composition, is abundantly frequent in Shakespeare's style.

DOCUMENTS MENTIONING WILLIAM SHAKESPEARE WHICH ARE EITHER SPURIOUS OR RELATING TO A NAMESAKE OF THE POET

1589. Appeal of the sharers in the Blackfriars Theatre to the Privy Council, Shakespeare's name being twelfth in the list. Manuscript published by Collier in *New Facts*, 1835. The date is quite inconsistent with what we know of Shakespeare's interest in the Blackfriars Theatre.[1]

1596. July. List of inhabitants of Liberty of Southwark, Shakespeare being sixth. Printed in Collier's *Life of Shakespeare,* 1858. Malone quoted a now missing memorandum of Alleyn, indicating Shakespeare's residence 'near the Bear Garden' in Southwark (Lee, *Life of Shakespeare,* p. 274). Compare document XIV, Note, p. 20.

1596. Petition of owners and players of Blackfriars Theatre to Privy Council. Shakespeare's name fifth. Printed in Collier's *History of English Dramatic Poetry,* 1831, i. 298-300. No evidence that Shakespeare's company played in Blackfriars before 1610.

1596. List of Shareholders in Blackfriars Theatre. Shakespeare listed as having four shares worth nearly a thousand pounds. MS. printed by Collier in *New Facts*, 1835. Spurious on the face of it.

1596? Letter signed H. S. (ostensibly Southampton)

---

1 For facsimiles and discussion of the forgeries ascribed to Collier see C. M. Ingleby, *A Complete View of the Shakspere Controversy*, 1861, pp. 241 ff.

asking Egerton's protection for Blackfriars players, particularly Burbage and Shakespeare. Collier, *New Facts*. Manifest forgery.

1600. March. Authentic document relating to suit by William Shakespeare against John Clayton of Bedfordshire for a debt of seven pounds contracted May 22, 1592. Judgment for Shakespeare with twenty shillings costs. No sufficient reason for identifying this Shakespeare with the poet. Cf. Lee, *Life of Shakespeare,* p. 321; Mrs. Stopes, *Shakespeare's Industry,* pp. 259, 262.

1603. Oct. 3. 'Mr. Shakespeare of the Globe' mentioned in letter from Mrs. Alleyn to her husband. Printed by Collier, *Memoirs of Edward Alleyn,* 1841, p. 63. Spurious.

1604. Apr. 9. Shakespeare named in list of players appended to Privy Council letter to Lord Mayor. Printed by Collier, ibid. p. 68. Spurious.

1604. July. Suit of William Shakespeare against Philip Rogers in Stratford court for debt on malt. Document printed by Halliwell-Phillipps, *Outlines,* ii. 77 f. Cf. Mrs. Stopes, *Shakespeare's Industry,* p. 263: 'There was another William Shakespeare . . . born at Rowington in 1564, whose trade was the selling of malt.'

1605. Sept. 23. William Shakspere listed as a trained soldier in a Rowington muster roll. Probably refers to the above.

1609. Apr. 8. Shakespeare named in list of taxpayers in Southwark. Printed in Collier's *Memoirs of Edward Alleyn,* 1841, pp. 90-92. Spurious.

1609 [1610]. Jan. 4. Warrant appointing Robert Daborne, William Shakespeare, etc., instructors of the Children's Revels company. Printed in Collier's *New Facts*, 1835. Certainly spurious.

THE CHIEF CONTEMPORARY ALLUSIONS TO SHAKESPEARE'S PLAYS[1]

I. *1 Henry VI*, 1592.

From Thomas Nashe, *Pierce Penniless, his Supplication to the Devil*, 1592.

How would it have joyed brave Talbot, the terror of the French, to think that after he had lien two hundred years in his tomb he should triumph again on the stage, and have his bones new embalmed with the tears of ten thousand spectators at least (at several times), who in the tragedian that represents his person imagine they behold him fresh bleeding!

NOTE. This alludes to the sensational success of the play of *Harry the Sixth* at the Rose Theatre in the spring of 1592. It is improbable that Shakespeare had any part in this piece, which he later expanded into *1 Henry VI*.

II. *The Comedy of Errors*, 1594.

From Henry Helmes[?], *Gesta Grayorum*, an account of the proceedings at Gray's Inn, London, on the night of December 28, 1594.

. . . And after such sports, a Comedy of Errors (like to Plautus his Menechmus) was played by the players. So that night was begun and continued to the end in nothing but confusion and errors; whereupon it was ever afterwards called The Night of Errors.

[1] For Meres' allusions and notes of court performances, see *ante*, pp. 25-26, 50-51.

III. *Love's Labour's Lost,* 1598, 1605.

(A) From Robert Tofte, *The Month's Mind of a Melancholy Lover,* 1598.

> *Love's Labour Lost: I once did see a play*
> *Ycleped so, so called to my pain,*
> *Which I to hear to my small joy did stay,*
> *Giving attendance on my froward dame.*
> *My misgiving mind presaging to me ill,*
> *Yet was I drawn to see it 'gainst my will.*
>
> *Each actor played in cunning wise his part,*
> *But chiefly those entrapt in Cupid's snare . . .*

(B) Letter of Sir Walter Cope to Lord Cranborne (Sir Robert Cecil), 1604/5.

Sir,

I have sent and been all this morning hunting for players, jugglers, and such kind of creatures, but find them hard to find; wherefore leaving notes for them to seek me, Burbage is come and says there is no new play that the Queen hath not seen, but they have revived an old one, called Love's Labour Lost, which for wit and mirth he says will please her exceedingly. And this is appointed to be played to-morrow night at my Lord of Southampton's, unless you send a writ to remove the corpus cum causa to your house in Strand.[1] Burbage is my messenger, ready attending your pleasure.

> *Yours most humbly,*
>
> WALTER COPE.

---

[1] I.e. unless you prefer to invite us to use your house in the Strand for the performance.

IV. *Julius Cæsar*, 1599, 1601.

(A) From the manuscript diary of Thomas Platter, a Swiss visitor to London in 1599.[1]

On Sept. 21 after lunch, at about two o'clock, I went with my company across the water [River Thames, and there] saw in the straw-thatched house [the Globe] the tragedy of the first emperor, Julius Cæsar, quite excellently acted by about fifteen persons. At the end of the comedy they danced according to their custom perfectly beautifully, two dressed in men's and two in women's clothes[2] . . . And so every day at two o'clock in the afternoon in the city of London two, sometimes even three, comedies are performed at different places . . . then those who perform best, they have the most auditors. The places are built in such a way that they play on a raised platform, and every one can well see all.

(B) From John Weever, *The Mirror of Martyrs*, 1601.

The many-headed multitude were drawn
By Brutus' speech that Cæsar was ambitious.

[1] Translated from the original German as printed by G. Binz, *Anglia*, 1899, pp. 456 ff.: 'Den 21 Septembris, nach dem Imbissessen, etwan vmb zwey vhren, bin ich mitt meiner geselschaft vber dz wasser gefahren, haben in dem streuwinen Dachhaus die Tragedy vom ersten Keyser Julio Caesare mitt ohngefahr 15 personen sehen gar artlich agieren; zu endt der Comedien dantzeten sie ihrem gebrauch nach gar vberausz zierlich, ye zwen in mannes vndt 2 in weiber kleideren angethan, wunderbahrlich mitt einanderen . . . vnndt werden also alle tag vmb 2 vhren nach mittag in der stadt London zwo, biszweilen auch drey Comedien an vnderschiedenen örteren gehalten, damitt einer den anderen lustig mache, dann welche sich am besten verhalten, die haben auch zum meisten Zuhörer. Die örter sindt dergestalt erbauwen, dasz sie auf einer erhöchten brüge spilen, vnndt yederman alles woll sehen kan.'
[2] This alludes to the *jig* which customarily concluded an Elizabethan play.

> *When eloquent Mark Antony had shown*
> *His virtues, who but Brutus then was vicious?*

V. *Henry IV*, 1599, 1600.

(A) Prologue to *Sir John Oldcastle*, 1599.[1]

> *It is no pamper'd glutton we present,*
> *Nor aged counselor to youthful sin,*
> *But one whose virtue shone above the rest,*
> *A valiant martyr and a virtuous peer.*
> *. . . Let fair truth be grac'd,*
> *Since forg'd invention former time defac'd.*

(B) Letter from Sir Charles Percy to a London friend, 1600?[2]

Mr. Carlington,

I am here so pestered with country business that I shall not be able as yet to come to London. If I stay here long in this fashion, at my return I think you will find me so dull that I shall be taken for Justice Silence or Justice Shallow; wherefore I am to entreat you that you will take pity of me, and as occurrences shall serve to send me such news from time to time as shall happen—the knowledge of which, though perhaps they will not exempt me from the opinion of a Justice Shallow at London, yet, I assure you, they will make

1 Acted in this year and published in 1600. The prologue gibes at Falstaff in his original name of Oldcastle. The text of the play contains two references to Falstaff: 'King [Henry V] . . . Where the devil are all my old thieves that were wont to keep this walk? Falstaff, the villain, is so fat he cannot get on's horse, but methinks Poins and Peto should be stirring hereabouts.'

'. . . Because he [the King] once robbed me before I fell to the trade myself; when that foul villainous guts that led him to all that roguery was in's company there, that Falstaff.'

2 Sir Charles Percy was probably a personal acquaintance of Shakespeare. He was one of the chief conspirators in Essex's insurrection in 1601, and seems to have been the person who arranged for the performance of *Richard II* as a prelude to the rising. See documents quoted in VI, below.

me pass for a very sufficient gentleman in Gloucester-shire. . . .

Your assured friend,

CHARLES PERCY

Dumbleton in Gloucestershire
this 27 of December.

(C) Postscript to Letter from Countess of South-ampton to her husband, dated Chartley, 8th July.[1]

All the news I can send you that I think will make you merry is that I read in a letter from London that Sir John Falstaff is by his mistress, Dame Pintpot, made father of a goodly miller's thumb, a boy that's all head and very little body; but this is a secret.

(D) From anonymous letter in a collection made by Sir Toby Matthews. Approximate date, 1600-1610. The writer is deploring the miscarriage of one of his earlier epistles.

For I must tell you I never dealt so freely with you in any; and (as that excellent author, Sir John Falstaff, says) what for your business, news, device, foolery, and liberty, I never dealt better since I was a man.[2]

VI. *Richard II*, 1601.

(A) Testimony of Sir Gelly Merrick, one of the participants in the Earl of Essex's insurrection.

The examination of Sir Gelly Merrick, Knight, taken the 17th of February, 1600 [i.e. 1601]. *He saith that upon Saturday last was sennight he dined*

1 The year is not indicated. Lady Southampton was residing at Chartley in July, 1599.
2 Cf. *I Henry IV*, II. iv. 190: 'I never dealt better since I was a man.'

*at Gunter's in the company of the Lord Monteagle,
Sir Christopher Blount, Sir Charles Percy, Ellis Jones,
and Edward Bushell, and who else he remembereth
not. And after dinner that day, and at the motion of
Sir Charles Percy and the rest, they went all together
to the Globe over the water where the Lord Chamberlain's men use to play, and were there somewhat
before the play began, Sir Charles telling them that the
play would be of Harry the Fourth.*[1] *Whether Sir
John Davies were there or not this examinate cannot
tell, but he said he would be there if he could. He cannot tell who procured that play to be played at that
time except it were Sir Charles Percy, but as he
thinketh it was Sir Charles Percy. Then he was at the
same play, and came in somewhat after it was begun;
and the play was of King Harry the Fourth and of
the killing of King Richard the Second, played by the
Lord Chamberlain's players.*

(B) Testimony of Shakespeare's partner and
friend, Augustine Phillips.

*The examination of Augustine Phillips, servant unto
the Lord Chamberlain and one of his players, taken
the 18th of February, 1600, upon his oath. He saith
that upon Friday last was sennight, or Thursday, Sir
Charles Percy, Sir Joscelin Percy, and the Lord
Monteagle, with some three more, spake to some of the
players in the presence of this examinate to have the
play of the deposing and killing of King Richard the
Second to be played the Saturday next, promising to
get them forty shillings more than their ordinary to*

1 Probably an equivocation. Shakespeare's *Richard II* does, of
course, introduce Henry IV, but Percy's hearers would assume that
he was taking them to see one of the two parts of *King Henry IV.*

*play it—where this examinate and his fellows were de-
termined to have played some other play, holding that
play of King Richard to be so old and so long out of
use as that they should have small or no company at
it. But at their request this examinate and his fellows
were content to play it the Saturday, and had their
forty shillings more than their ordinary for it, and so
played it accordingly.*

(C) Conversation between Queen Elizabeth and
William Lambard, the antiquary, at Greenwich Palace,
August 4, 1601, as reported by Lambard.

Queen. . . . I am Richard II. Know ye not that?
*W. L. Such a wicked imagination was determined
and attempted by a most unkind Gent. [Essex], the
most adorned creature that ever your Majesty made.*
*Her Majesty. He that will forget God will also
forget his benefactors. This tragedy was played
forty times in open streets and houses.*

NOTE. Though doubt has often been expressed, it is
morally certain that it was Shakespeare's *Richard II*
which was acted by way of preparing people's minds
for the Essex insurrection.

VII. *Richard III*, 1602.

Scene from second part of *The Return from Parnassus*, produced at Cambridge, ca. Christmas, 1602.
Burbage the actor is examining the qualifications of
the student Philomusus, who wishes to go on the stage.

*Burbage. I like your face and the proportion of
your body for Richard the Third. I pray, Mr.
Philomusus, let me see you act a little of it.*

Philomusus. '*Now is the winter of our discontent*
                         Made glorious summer by the sun of
                         York.'
Burbage.   Very well, I assure you!

VIII. *Twelfth Night,* 1602.

Extract from diary of John Manningham,[1] February
2, 1602, alluding to performance in the Middle Temple.

At our feast we had a play called Twelve Night, or
What you Will, *much like the* Comedy of Errors *or*
Menechmi *in Plautus, but most like and near to that in
Italian called* Inganni. *A good practice in it to make
the steward believe his lady widow was in love with
him by counterfeiting a letter in general terms, telling
him what she liked best in him, and prescribing his
gesture in smiling, his apparel, &c., and then when he
came to practice making him believe they took him to
be mad.*

IX. *Hamlet* and *Richard II* acted at sea, 1607, 1608.

Notes of Captain William Keeling of the East India
Co. ship *Dragon,* off Sierra Leone, 1607, 1608.[2]

*September 5.   I sent the interpreter, according to
his desire, aboard the* Hector, *where he broke fast and
after came aboard me, where we gave the tragedy of*
Hamlet.
*September 30.   Captain Hawkins dined with me,
where my companions acted* King Richard the Second.
March[3] *31.   I invited Captain Hawkins to a fish*

---

1 Compare ante, p. 39.
2 These notes were first printed in 1849 by Thomas Rundall from
a manuscript not now available.   Their authenticity is vindicated by
F. S. Boas, *Shakespeare and the Universities,* 1923, pp. 84 ff.
3 The date was printed by Rundall as 'September 31' (*sic*), but
corrected in manuscript, probably by Rundall, as above.

dinner, and had Hamlet *acted aboard me; which I permit to keep my people from idleness and unlawful games or sleep.*

X. *Pericles*, 1609-1629.

(A) Allusion in anonymous poem called *Pimlyco, or Run Red-Cap*, 1609.

> *Amazed I stood, to see a crowd*
> *Of civil throats stretched out so loud,*
> *As at a new play all the rooms*
> *Did swarm with gentles mixed with grooms;*
> *So that I truly thought all these*
> *Came to see* Shore[1] *or* Pericles.

(B) From Prologue to Robert Taylor's play, *The Hog hath Lost his Pearl*, 1614.

> *And if it prove so happy as to please,*
> *We'll say 'tis fortunate, like* Pericles.

(C) Ben Jonson, *Ode to Himself*, written after the failure of his play, *The New Inn*, in 1629.

> *No doubt some mouldy tale,*
> *Like* Pericles, *and stale*
> *As the shrieve's crusts, and nasty as his fish-*
> *Scraps, out of every dish*
> *Thrown forth and raked into the common tub,*
> *May keep up the Play-club.*
> *There sweepings do as well*
> *As the best-ordered meal:*
> *For who the relish of these guests will fit*
> *Needs sets them but the almsbasket of wit.*

---

[1] Alluding probably to Thomas Heywood's popular play of *Edward IV*, in two parts, which dealt largely with the sentimental tale of Jane Shore, that king's mistress.

NOTE. The immense and undeserved popularity of *Pericles* was proverbial through all the long period represented by these quotations.

XI. *Othello,* 1610.

Extract from the diary of Prince Lewis Frederick of Würtemberg, kept by his secretary, H. J. Wurmsser, chronicling his visit to England in 1610.

Monday, April 30, 1610. His Excellency went to the Globe, the usual place where comedies are played. There was represented the history of the Moor of Venice.[1]

XII. *Macbeth,* 1610.

Entry in Dr. Simon Forman's Diary, April 20, 1610.

In Macbeth at the Globe, 1610, the 20. of April, Saturday, there was to be observed, first, how Macbeth and Banquo, two noblemen of Scotland, riding through a wood, there stood before them three women, fairies or nymphs, and saluted Macbeth, saying three times unto him: Hail, Macbeth, King of Codon [sic], for thou shalt be a king, but shalt beget no kings, etc. Then said Banquo: What, all to Macbeth and nothing to me? Yes, said the nymphs, Hail to thee, Banquo; thou shalt beget kings, yet be no king. And so they departed and came to the court of Scotland, to Duncan King of Scots, and it was in the days of Edward the Confessor. And Duncan bade them both kindly welcome, and made Macbeth forthwith Prince of Northumberland and sent him home to his own castle, and appointed Macbeth to provide for him, for he would

---

1 Translated. 'Lundi, 30. S. E. alla au Globe, lieu ordinaire ou l'on joue les commedies, y fut representé l'histoire du More de Venise.'

*sup with him the next day at night, and did so. And
Macbeth contrived to kill Duncan, and through the
persuasion of his wife did that night murder the king
in his own castle, being his guest; and there were
many prodigies seen that night and the day before.
And when Macbeth had murdered the king, the blood
on his hands could not be washed off by any means,
nor from his wife's hands, which handled the bloody
daggers in hiding them, by which means they became
both much amazed and affronted. The murder being
known, Duncan's two sons fled, the one to England,
the [other to] Wales, to save themselves. They being
fled, they were supposed guilty of the murder of their
father, which was nothing so. Then was Macbeth
crowned King; and then—for fear of Banquo, his old
companion, that he should beget kings, but be no
king himself—he contrived the death of Banquo and
caused him to be murdered on the way as he rode. The
next night, being at supper with his noblemen whom
he had bid to a feast, to the which also Banquo should
have come, he began to speak of noble Banquo and to
wish that he were there. And as he thus did, standing
up to drink a carouse to him, the ghost of Banquo
came and sat down in his chair behind him. And he,
turning about to sit down again, saw the ghost of
Banquo, which fronted him so that he fell into a great
passion of fear and fury, uttering many words about
his murder, by which, when they heard that Banquo
was murdered, they suspected Macbeth. Then Macduff[1] fled to England to the king's son, and so they
raised an army and came into Scotland, and at Dun-
ston [i.e. Dunsinane] Anyse [i.e. Malcolm] over-
threw Macbeth. In the meantime, while Macduff was*

1 Spelled Mack Dove in the manuscript.

in England, Macbeth slew Macduff's wife and chil-
dren, and after in the battle Macduff slew Macbeth.
Observe also how Macbeth's queen did rise in the night
in her sleep and walk, and talked and confessed all,
and the doctor noted her words.

NOTE. Forman naturally commits many errors of detail, but his terse, biblical narrative gives an unrivaled
impression of what a contemporary audience got from
a play of Shakespeare.

XIII. *Cymbeline*, 1610-1611.

Undated entry in Forman's Diary, probably belonging to the months between XII and XIV.

Of Cimbalin King of England. Remember also the
story of Cymbeline, King of England in Lucius' time:
how Lucius came from Octavius Cæsar for tribute,
and being denied [Cæsar] after sent Lucius with a
great army of soldiers, who landed at Milford Haven,
and after were vanquished by Cymbeline and Lucius
taken prisoner. And all by means of three outlaws,
of the which two of them were the sons of Cymbeline,
stolen from him when they were but two years old by
an old man whom Cymbeline banished; and he kept
them as his own sons twenty years with him in a cave.
And how one of them slew Cloten, that was the Queen's
son, going to Milford Haven to seek the love[1] of
Innogen, the King's daughter, whom he had banished
also for loving his daughter. And how the Italian that
came from her love conveyed himself into a chest, and
said it was a chest of plate sent from her love and
others to be presented to the King; and in the deepest
of the night, she being asleep, he opened the chest

[1] I.e. lover (Posthumus).

*and came forth of it, and viewed her in her bed and
the marks of her body, and took away her bracelet,
and after accused her of adultery to her love, &c;
and in the end how he came with the Romans into
England, and was taken prisoner, and after revealed
to Innogen, who had turned herself into man's apparel
and fled to meet her love at Milford Haven, and
chanced to fall on the cave in the woods where her two
brothers were. And how, by eating a sleeping dram,
they thought she had been dead and laid her in the
woods, and the body of Cloten by her in her love's
apparel that he left behind him; and how she was
found by Lucius, &c.*

XIV. *The Winter's Tale*, 1611.

Entry in Forman's Diary, May 15, 1611.

*In the Winter's Tale at the Globe, 1611, the 15 of
May, Wednesday.—Observe there how Leontes, the
King of Sicilia, was overcome with jealousy of his
wife with the King of Bohemia, his friend that came
to see him, and how he contrived his death and would
have had his cupbearer to have poisoned—who gave
the King of Bohemia warning thereof and fled with him
to Bohemia. Remember also how he sent to the oracle
of Apollo, and the answer of Apollo that she was guilt-
less and that the king was jealous, &c., and how, except
the child was found again that was lost, the king
should die without issue: for the child was carried
into Bohemia and there laid in a forest, and brought
up by a shepherd; and the King of Bohemia his son
married that wench. And how they fled into Sicilia
to Leontes, and the shepherd having showed the letter
of the nobleman by whom Leontes sent that child and*

the jewels found about her, she was known to be Leontes' daughter and was then sixteen years old. Remember also the rogue that came in all tottered like Coll Pipci,[1] and how he feigned him sick and to have been robbed of all that he had, and how he cozened the poor man of all his money, and after came to the sheep-shear with a pedlar's pack and there cozened them again of all their money; and how he changed apparel with the King of Bohemia his son, and then how he turned courtier, &c. Beware of trusting feigned beggars or fawning fellows.

XV. *Henry VIII*, 1613.

Letter of Thomas Lorkins to Sir Thomas Puckering, June 30, 1613.

London, this last of June, 1613.

No longer since than yesterday, while Burbage his company were acting at the Globe the play of Henry VIII, and there shooting off certain chambers in way of triumph, the fire catched and fastened upon the thatch of the house, and there burned so furiously as it consumed the whole house, and all in less than two hours, the people having enough to do to save themselves.[2]

XVI. *The Tempest* and *The Winter's Tale*, 1614.

From Induction to Ben Jonson's *Bartholomew Fair*.

If there be never a servant-monster i' the Fair, who can help it, he says; nor a nest of antics? He is loath to make Nature afraid in his plays, like those that

---

1 Tattered like Coltpixie (a roguish sprite).
2 For a more detailed account of this fire, written two days later by Sir Henry Wotton, see the edition of *Henry VIII* in this series, pp. 150 f.

beget Tales, Tempests, *and suchlike drolleries—to mix his head with other men's heels.*

NOTE. It is virtually certain that 'servant-monster' is an allusion to Caliban; and it is probable that by 'a nest of antics' and 'suchlike drolleries' Jonson means the tricks of Autolycus and the anti-masks introduced into both *The Winter's Tale* and *The Tempest*. Another gibe at the popularity of Caliban is probably found in a line of the Prologue (1616) to Jonson's *Every Man in his Humour:*

'You that have so graced monsters, may like men.'[1]

[1] The Revels Accounts for 1611 record that the King's Players gave court performances of *The Tempest*, 'at Whitehall before the King's Majesty' on November 1, and of 'a play called The Winter's Night's Tale' on November 5. Both were repeated at court in 1613.

THE PRINTING OF SHAKESPEARE'S
WORKS.

Of the forty works commonly ascribed to Shakespeare nineteen—including *Venus and Adonis, Lucrece,* the Sonnets, and sixteen plays—were published in separate, quarto editions previous to the date of his retirement, about 1611. Another play, *Othello,* was first published in quarto in 1622. The remaining twenty plays first appeared in the collected Folio edition of the poet's dramatic works in 1623.

Normally one finds, about the date of the first publication of each of the works printed in quarto, an entry in the register of the Stationers' (printers' and booksellers') Company of London, establishing the publisher's copyright in the work and his authority from the censors to print. There are two plays, however—*Romeo and Juliet* and *Love's Labour's Lost*—for which no entry or license prior to publication has been found. Conversely, two other plays were entered on the Stationers' Register (one of them conditionally) which remained unprinted till included in the Folio. These were *As You Like It* (entered, 'to be stayed,' Aug. 4, 1600) and *Antony and Cleopatra* (entered, May 20, 1608).

The quarto editions are good, bad, and indifferent. Among the best are the first editions of *Venus and Adonis* and *Lucrece,* probably printed under Shakespeare's personal supervision; the second editions of *Romeo and Juliet* and *Hamlet* and the first of *1 Henry IV* and *Love's Labour's Lost,* issued by special authority of Shakespeare's company. The worst of the bad quartos are the first editions of *Romeo and Juliet* and *Hamlet* and all the quartos of *Henry V,* the *Merry Wives,* and *Pericles,* the text of which evidently depends upon truncated and very inexact reconstructions of the acted plays, obtained against the will of the company. Another group of bad quartos is a set of spurious editions issued in 1619 by Thomas Pavier with false earlier dates; these include the second editions of *The Merchant of Venice, A Midsummer Night's Dream,* and *King Lear,* and the third edition of *Henry V.* To the same group belong also the 1619 *Pericles* and *Merry Wives,* the dates of which have not been falsified.

Elizabethan printing was of indifferent quality, and the best printers of the day were not the ones who brought out the cheap play quartos. Misprints are numerous and differences of text frequently appear in different copies of the same quarto, owing to the slovenly habit of waiting to correct errors till they were casually observed as the sheets were being printed off. The tendency is for the text of a play to degenerate through the series of editions, each later quarto being printed from the one immediately preceding it and adding typographical errors to those its predecessor had accumulated. Except in the case of the two poems, it is unlikely that Shakespeare exercised supervision over the printing of any of his works. Some were undoubtedly printed fraudulently and without the aid of an authoritative manuscript.

Of the twenty titles which appeared in print before 1623, *Titus Andronicus* and *Henry V* are anonymous in all the quartos, and Shakespeare's name appears for the first time on the title-page of certain copies of the fourth, undated, edition of *Romeo and Juliet.*[1] The

---

[1] The title-page in this edition varies in different copies, some having and some omitting Shakespeare's name.

second quartos of *Richard II, Richard III,* and *1 Henry IV* are the earliest to indicate his authorship, the first quartos of these plays being anonymous. Otherwise Shakespeare is marked as the author in the first and all subsequent editions.

The Folio, with all its faults, is a better printed book than the average of the quartos. For twenty of the plays it is, as said, our sole authority. For the other sixteen plays[1] the Folio sometimes follows an entirely independent and superior manuscript, as in *Richard III, Henry V,* and *Merry Wives;* but more often shows that it was printed from one of the quarto editions, with the text corrected, expanded, or cut for the actors' needs. Where a number of quarto editions had appeared (e.g. *Romeo and Juliet* and *1 Henry IV*), it was one of the later and typographically less correct ones which was so used. The chief textual embarrassments of Shakespeare students arise from these cases, where the 'good' quartos and the Folio offer alternative readings. *Richard II,* the two parts of *Henry IV, Hamlet, Lear, Troilus and Cressida,* and *Othello* are the plays in which this conflict of authority is most apparent.

1 The Folio does not include the Poems, Sonnets, or *Pericles.*

LIST OF QUARTO EDITIONS OF SHAKESPEARE'S WORKS BEFORE 1623

	Entry in Stationers' Register	Q1	Q2	Q3	Q4	Q5	Q6	Q7	Q8	Q9
Venus and Adonis	Apr. 18, 1593	1593	1594	?[1]	1596	1599	1599	1602	1617	1620
Lucrece	May 9, 1594	1594	1598	1600	1607	1616				
Titus Andronicus	Feb. 6, 1594	1594	1600	1611						
Richard III	Aug. 29, 1597	1597	1598	1602	1605	1612	1622			
Richard II	Oct. 29, 1597	1597	1598	1598	1608[2]	1615				
Romeo and Juliet ⎫	No entry of either	1597	1599	1609	n.d.					
Love's Labour's Lost ⎭	till Jan. 22, 1607	?[3]	1598							
1 Henry IV	Feb. 25, 1598	1598[4]	1599	1604	1608	1613	1622			
Merchant of Venice	July 17, 1598[5]	1600	'1600' (1619)[6]							
Henry V	Aug. 4, 1600	1600	1602	'1608' (1619)[6]						
Much Ado about Nothing	Aug. 4, 1600[5]	1600								
2 Henry IV	Aug. 23, 1600	1600								
Midsummer Night's Dream	Oct. 8, 1600	1600	'1600' (1619)[6]							
Merry Wives of Windsor	Jan. 18, 1602	1602	1619							
Hamlet	July 26, 1602	1603	1604 1605[7]	1611	n.d.					
Lear	Nov. 26, 1607	1608	'1608' (1619)[6]							
Sonnets	May 20, 1609	1609								
Troilus and Cressida	Feb. 7, 1603[5]	1609[2]								
Pericles	May 20, 1608	1609	1609	1611	1619					
Othello	Oct. 6, 1621	1622								

1 Only one fragmentary copy known, from which title-page and date are missing.

2 There are two issues of this edition with differing title-pages only. (The later issue of Troilus and Cressida adds a preface.)

3 No copy known, but there is reason to believe that the 1598 edition was not the first.

4 There is a fragmentary copy thought to be earlier than this.

5 Provisional entries. Later entries of Merchant of Venice, Oct. 28, 1600; Much Ado, Aug. 28, 1600; Troilus and Cressida, Jan. 28, 1609.

6 Spurious edition bearing false date, really printed in 1619.

7 Some copies of the second edition of Hamlet are dated 1604, others 1605.

CHRONOLOGICAL ORDER OF SHAKE-SPEARE'S WORKS

The order and approximate date of composition of the plays written during the last half of Shakespeare's career have been fixed with a good deal of definiteness. From *Henry V, Julius Cæsar,* and *Much Ado,* all produced about 1599-1600, a marked development in mannerisms and style, and the existence of a considerable body of contemporary allusions, enable critics to arrange the sequence of maturer plays in a series not likely to be fundamentally shaken. For the earlier plays and the sonnets this is not true. We cannot determine with any approach to certainty the time or manner in which Shakespeare began to write. Biographers like to infer that his poetical work commenced immediately after he came to London—say, in 1587-1588—or even before he left Stratford. Some assume that he began with narrative poetry, e.g. *Venus and Adonis,* others with an independent play like *The Comedy of Errors,* others as reviser of old plays like *Titus Andronicus* and *Henry VI.* There is, however, no positive evidence that any line of his writing was in existence before 1592, though the circumstantial evidence is strong against the possibility that the great quantity of writing we know him to have achieved by 1597, and the vast artistic progress we know him to have made, can have been the product of only five years.

Another fact which makes it impossible to date with positiveness Shakespeare's earlier plays is that Elizabethan dramatic fashions changed very rapidly during the period from 1590 till 1600 and that Shakespeare's

Date of composition (?)	Comedies	Histories	Tragedies	Non
1588-1594	Comedy of Errors			
1590	Love's Labour's Lost			
1591	Two Gentlemen of Verona			
1592		Henry VI, Pts. II & III		
1592				Venus a
1593-1594				Lucrece
1593				
1594			Titus Andronicus	
1594		Richard III		
1594	Midsummer Night's Dream			
1595		Richard II		
1595			Romeo and Juliet	
1595-1596		King John		
1594-1600				Sonnet
1596	Merchant of Venice			
1596	Taming of the Shrew			
1597		1 Henry IV		
1598		2 Henry IV		
1599		Henry V		
1599		Henry VI, Pt. I		
1599			Julius Cæsar	
1599-1600	Merry Wives of Windsor			
1600	Much Ado about Nothing			
1600	As You Like It			
1601	Twelfth Night			
1601			Hamlet	
1602			Troilus and Cressida	
1603	Measure for Measure			
1596-1606	All's Well that Ends Well			
1604			Othello	
1605			Lear	
1606			Macbeth	
1607			Timon of Athens	
1607			Antony and Cleopatra	
1606-1608	Pericles			
1608-1609			Coriolanus	
1610	Cymbeline			
1610-1611	Winter's Tale			
1611	Tempest			
1613		Henry VIII		

Chief Source	First definite mention	First Printed	Conjectural dates of Fleay	Alden	Adams
Plautus	Dec. 28, 1594 (Helmes)	1623	1594	1590-1591	1588-1589
Unknown	1598 (Meres)	1598		1590-1591	1592
Montemayor	1598 (Meres)	1623	1591-1595	1591-1592	1592-1594
Old plays, Holinshed	Sept., 1592 (Greene)	1623		1590-1592	1592
Ovid	Apr. 18, 1593 (S. R.)	1593			1592-1593
Ovid, Livy	May 9, 1594 (S. R.)	1594			1593-1594
?Older play	Jan. 23, 1594 (performance)	1594			
Holinshed	Oct. 19, 1597 (S. R.)	1597	1594	1592-1593	1595
Unknown	1598 (Meres)	1600	1595	1593-1595	1596
Holinshed	Aug. 29, 1597 (S. R.)	1597	1595	1594-1595	1595
Arthur Brooke	July, 1596-Apr., 1597 (Ld. Hunsdon's Co.)	1597	1595-1596	1594-1597	1593-1596
Older plays	1598 (Meres)	1623	1596	1592-1593	1595
	1598 (Meres)	1609			1592-1594
G. Fiorentino	1598 (Meres)	1600	1596-1597	1594-1596	1597
Older play	? ? ?	1623	1603	1596-1597	1597
Older play, Holinshed	Feb. 25, 1598 (S. R.)	1598	1597	1597-1598	1597
Holinshed	Aug. 23, 1600 (S. R.)	1600	1597-1598	1597-1598	1597-1598
Holinshed	Aug. 4, 1600 (S. R.)	1600	1599	1599	1598
Older play, Holinshed		1623		1590-1592	1594-1595, 1598-1599
Plutarch	Sept. 21, 1599 (T. Platter's diary); 1599-1601 (Weever)	1623	1600	1599-1600	1599
Unknown	Jan. 18, 1602 (S. R.)	1602	1600	1598-1599	1598
Bandello	Aug. 4, 1600 (S. R.)	1600	1597-1598	1599	1599
Lodge	Aug. 4, 1600 (S. R.)	1623	1599	1599-1600	1599
Barnabe Rich	Feb. 2, 1602 (Manningham)	1623	1601-1602	1601	1599
Older play	July 26, 1602 (S. R.)	1603	1603	1602-1604	1601
Chaucer, Caxton	Feb. 7, 1603 (S. R.)	1609	1602	1601-1602	1602
Older plays	Dec. 26, 1604 (Court performance)	1623	1604	1603	1603-1604
Boccaccio	?1598 (Meres)	1623	1593-1601	1602-1604	1596, 1600-1
Cinthio	Nov. 1, 1604 (Court performance)	1622	1604	1604	1604
Older play, Sidney	Dec. 26, 1606 (Court performance)	1608	1605	1605-1606	1605
Holinshed	Apr. 20, 1610 (Forman's diary)	1623	1606	1606	1606
Plutarch, older play?	? ? ?	1623	1606-1607	1607-1608	1607
Plutarch	May 20, 1608 (S. R.)	1623	1607	1607-1608	1607
Gower	May 20, 1608 (S. R.)	1609	1608	1607-1608	1607
Plutarch	1609? (allusion in Jonson's Silent Woman)	1623	1608	1609	1608-1609
Holinshed, Boccaccio	1610? (undated note in Forman)	1623	1609	1610	1609-1610
Greene	May 15, 1611 (Forman)	1623	1610	1611	1610-1611
Contemporary pamphlets, etc.	Nov. 1, 1611 (Court performance)	1623	1610	1611	1611
Holinshed	June 29, 1613 (Globe Theatre fire)	1623	1613	1612	1613

personal taste and powers developed even more. The conditions of the day led to radical revision of plays, almost as often as they were revived, to suit the changing manners of the theatre and the playwright. Some of Shakespeare's earlier works are therefore palimpsests, containing writing of several different periods, impossible to refer to a single point in the poet's development. *Love's Labour's Lost* and *All's Well that Ends Well* (probably originally presented under the title of *Love's Labour's Won*) are striking examples of this mixture of styles.

A list of Shakespeare's works, classified according to type, and arranged in conjectural chronological order follows. For purposes of comparison the dates assigned by three other critics, Mr. Fleay, Professor Alden, and Professor Adams, are added in the last three columns. Titles of works which are of doubtful or only partial authenticity are printed in italic.

SHAKESPEARE'S METRICAL
DEVELOPMENT

Shakespeare's use of poetry, and especially of blank verse, in his dramas shows a strikingly progressive development which is very important both in measuring his intellectual and artistic growth and in corroborating the dates of his various plays. The metrical tests, mainly worked out during the last part of the nineteenth century, require both judgment and imagination for effective use; but when so used they become an indispensable implement for the appreciation of the poet.

The chief facts established by the study of Shakespeare's use of metre are the following:

(A) In early plays Shakespeare secures variety and an ornate effect by much use of riming couplets, to which he also adds more elaborate metrical forms, such as the quatrain, six-line stanza, and sonnet. In later plays he depends increasingly upon unrelieved blank verse, finally discarding rime altogether, except in inserted songs.

(B) In earlier plays he sticks rather monotonously to the type line of exactly ten syllables. In later plays he gets variety by larger use of eleven-syllable (feminine-ending) and even twelve-syllable lines, which in *The Tempest* exceed the proportion of one in three.

(C) In earlier plays each line is ordinarily felt as a separate unit, its individuality being marked off by a pause at the end (end-stopped). In later plays this mechanical pattern is broken up by increasing employment of unstopped, or run-on, lines, where one flows into another without a break. In plays of the last period the proportion of unstopped lines is almost one in two.

(D) A special manifestation of the tendency toward unstopped lines, which appears in later plays, is the introduction of 'light' and 'weak' endings,[1] where the line ends, not simply without a punctuation point or logical pause, but in the middle of a prepositional phrase, between a subject pronoun and its verb, after an auxiliary verb (am, can, have, do, etc.) or a conjunction such as 'and,' 'or,' 'than,' etc. Here there is not only no logical pause, but the mechanical tendency to pause at the close of the line is definitely prohibited and the two verses completely agglutinated. Such lines barely exist in earlier plays, but become a marked mannerism after *Macbeth*.

(E) Another minor development illustrating Shakespeare's tendency to substitute flexibility for mechanical precision is the habit of ending speeches in the middle instead of at the close of a line. In earlier plays characters usually speak in blocks of complete ten-syllable verses; in later plays animation and naturalness are gained by frequently splitting a line between two speakers or leaving the last line of a speech incomplete.

Most metrical tests can never be mathematically precise, since the data they are based on—pronunciation, pause, punctuation—are in part a matter of personal taste and habit, and no two calculators will compile identical lists of statistics. Nor, even if the calculations could be made altogether mechanical and scientific, would the tests establish an absolutely accurate order of priority for the plays; for the trend on the poet's part was unconscious and instinctive, and was

1 *Light* endings are supposed to be less entirely incapable of stress than *weak*, but the distinction is shadowy.

subject to check or acceleration by the nature of the material he was working on. It is natural that in a fairy play like *A Midsummer Night's Dream* Shakespeare should use more rime than we should expect him to use in a psychological play of the same period; just as it is natural for him to use much more prose in *Coriolanus,* which deals largely with the Plebeians' view of life than in *Antony and Cleopatra,* where the tone is epic and aristocratic. There can, however, be no question about the validity of the general conclusions established by the metrical tests.

The net result of the changes which Shakespeare's manner of writing went through was the evolution of a type of blank verse uniquely expressive and powerful. The greatest development was made during the period of the great tragedies, from about 1601 till 1608. In this time he came to restrict himself practically solely, except in songs, to prose and blank verse, and his blank verse became steadily more independent of conventional patterns and more fluid in its movement. At the same time Shakespeare's diction grew bolder and more compressed, heavier with thought and more allusive. The contrast between his middle and his late style is aptly illustrated by two short passages, in *Julius Cæsar* and *Coriolanus* respectively, where the poet happens to describe the same scene, viz. a mob of vulgar Romans pressing to see the triumphant return of a successful general. This is in the style of 1599, workmanlike, very lucid, but still a little conventional:

'O you hard hearts, you cruel men of Rome,
Knew you not Pompey? Many a time and oft
Have you climb'd up to walls and battlements,
To towers and windows, yea, to chimney-tops,

Your infants in your arms, and there have sat
The livelong day, with patient expectation,
To see great Pompey pass the streets of Rome:
And when you saw his chariot but appear,
Have you not made a universal shout,
That Tiber trembled underneath her banks,
To hear the replication of your sounds
Made in her concave shores?
And do you now put on your best attire?
And do you now cull out a holiday?
And do you now strew flowers in his way,
That comes in triumph over Pompey's blood?'
(Julius Cæsar, I. i. 40-55)

The words are those of the Tribune Marullus. Note the marvelously different way in which the Tribune Brutus in *Coriolanus* says the same thing some nine years later:

'All tongues speak of him, and the bleared sights
Are spectacled to see him: your prattling nurse
Into a rapture lets her baby cry
While she chats him: the kitchen malkin pins
Her richest lockram 'bout her reechy neck,
Clambering the walls to eye him: stalls, bulks,
    windows
Are smother'd up, leads fill'd, and ridges hors'd
With variable complexions, all agreeing
In earnestness to see him: seld-shown flamens
Do press among the popular throngs, and puff
To win a vulgar station: our veil'd dames
Commit the war of white and damask in
Their nicely-gawded cheeks to the wanton spoil
Of Phoebus' burning kisses: such a pother
As if that whatsoever god who leads him

Were slily crept into his human powers,
And gave him graceful posture.'
                    (*Coriolanus*, II. i. 224-240)

The two passages are within a line of the same
length, and they are as nearly as possible identical
in the subject, setting, and attitude of the speaker.
The earlier one contains *one* double ending, *three* unstopped lines, and *one* word (*replication*) which might
possibly require explanation to modern school children.
The later passage has *six* double endings, *fourteen*
unstopped lines, and at least *sixteen* words used in
strange or obsolete senses. The speech in *Coriolanus*
also contains a typical specimen of the weak ending
(sixth line from close), and it concludes in the middle
of a line.

The following table gives metrical statistics for the
various plays.

Works of dubious or only partial authenticity are
indicated in italic. The statistics are given as counted
by Fleay,[1] König,[2] and Ingram.[3]

---

[1] *Trans. New Shakspere Society*, 1874, p. 16, for figures in the first
four columns.

[2] G. König, *Der Vers in Shaksperes Dramen*, 1888, pp. 131 ff. for
the percentages in columns 5, 6, 7, and 9. It will be observed that
the percentages of riming lines given by König in column 5 are in
many cases materially different from those which would be obtained
by using Fleay's count of riming and blank verse lines.

[3] J. K. Ingram, *Trans. New Shakspere Society*, 1874, pp. 442 ff.,
for figures in column 8.

Play	Total lines	Prose	Blank verse	Riming lines (5-ft.)	% Riming lines	% Feminine endings lines	% Run-on lines	No. light (weak) endings	% Speeches ending within line
Comedy of Errors	1770	240	1150	380	19.4	16.6	12.9	0	.6
Love's Labour's Lost	2789	1086	579	1028	62.2	7.7	18.4	3	10.
Two Gentlemen of Verona	2060	409	1510	116	6.5	18.4	12.4	0	5.8
1 Henry VI	2693	0	2379	314	10.	8.2	10.4	4	.5
2 Henry VI	3032	448	2562	122	2.9	13.7	11.4	3	1.1
3 Henry VI	2904	0	2749	155	3.4	13.7	12.	3	.9
Titus Andronicus	2525	43	2338	144	3.7	8.6	13.1	5	2.5
Richard III	3599	55	3374	170	3.5	19.5	13.2	2	2.9
Midsummer Night's Dream	2251	441	878	731	43.4	7.3	19.9	1	17.3
Richard II	2644	0	2107	537	18.6	11.	14.2	4	7.3
Romeo & Juliet	3002	405	2111	486	17.2	8.2	17.7	7	14.9
King John	2553	0	2403	150	5.5	6.3	21.5	7	12.1
Merchant of Venice	2705	673	1896	93	4.6	17.7	8.1	7	22.2
Taming of the Shrew	2671	516	1971	169	4.4	5.1	22.8	2	3.6
1 Henry IV	3170	1464	1622	84	2.7	5.1	21.4	2	14.2
2 Henry IV	3437	1860	1417	74	2.9	16.3	21.8	7	16.8
Henry V	3320	1531	1678	101	3.2	20.5	19.3	1	18.3
Julius Cæsar	2440	165	2241	34	1.2	19.7	20.1	10	20.3
Merry Wives of Windsor	3018	2703	227	69	6.4	27.2	19.3	1	20.5
Much Ado about Nothing	2823	2106	643	40	5.2	22.9	17.1	2	20.7
As You Like It	2904	1681	925	71	6.3	25.5	14.7	2	21.6
Twelfth Night	2684	1741	763	120	13.7	25.6	23.1	4	36.3
Hamlet	3924	1208	2490	81	2.7	22.6	27.4	8	51.6
Troilus and Cressida	3423	1186	2025	196	8.6	23.8	23.	6	31.3
Measure for Measure	2809	1134	1574	73	3.6	26.1	28.4	7	51.4
All's Well that Ends Well	2981	1453	1234	280	19.4	29.4	29.3	13	74.
Othello	3324	541	2672	86	3.2	28.1	29.3	8	41.4
Lear	3298	903	2238	74	3.4	28.5	29.3	6	60.9
Macbeth	1993	158	1588	118	5.8	26.3	36.6	23	77.2
Timon of Athens	2358	596	1560	184	8.5	24.7	32.5	30	62.8
Antony and Cleopatra	3064	255	2761	42	.7	26.5	43.3	99	77.5
Pericles	2386	418	1436	225	18.8	20.2	18.2	82	17.1
Coriolanus	3392	829	2521	42	.7	28.4	45.9	104	79.
Cymbeline	3448	638	2585	107	3.2	30.7	46.	130	85.
Winter's Tale	2758	844	1825	0	0.	32.9	37.5	100	87.6
Tempest	2068	458	1458	2	.1	35.4	41.5	67	84.5
Henry VIII	**2754**	**67**	**2613**	**16**	**.3**	**47.3**	**46.3**	**84**	**72.4**

SHAKESPEARE'S THEATRES[1]

The plays of Shakespeare were acted during his lifetime upon every variety of stage then existing. These differed in elegance, convenience, and even in the fundamental facilities for acting, to an extent which it is now hard to realize. They may be classified as follows:

A. Theatres in London and its environs.

  (a) Public Theatres.

    (1) The Inn-yards. Since the city authorities of London refused to countenance professional acting, regular theatres might not be built within the 'liberties' or district subject to municipal control. Hence the only public performances within the city proper[2] took place in the interior yards of inns, a time-honored scene of dramatic as well as acrobatic and pugilistic exhibitions. Five inn-yards were particularly noted in this way: that of the *Bell Savage* on Ludgate Hill, just west of the city wall; of the *Boar's Head,* Whitechapel, east of the city wall; of the *Cross Keys* and *Bell* in Gracechurch Street, and the *Bull* in Bishopsgate Street. The last three were all within the city wall and on a line leading from London Bridge on the south to Bishopsgate and the northern suburbs in which the 'Theatre' and 'Curtain' stood. Shakespeare's plays may have been occasionally performed in any of these. We know that his company, the Chamberlain's, acted regu-

1 For an extensive and admirable treatment of this subject see J. Q. Adams, *Shakespearean Playhouses,* 1917.
2 Very roughly speaking, within the circuit of the old city wall.

larly at the Cross Keys in the winter of 1594,[1] and that their predecessors, Lord Strange's men, played in the same inn-yard in 1589.

(2) Playhouses in Finsbury Fields, north of London Wall.

(i) The 'Theatre,' built in 1576 by James Burbage, father of Shakespeare's colleague, the great actor. This was the first building specially erected for the presentation of plays. It was on the edge of Finsbury Fields (or Moorfields), beyond Bishopsgate Street, in which ward Shakespeare lived (in St. Helen's parish) previous to 1597. This theatre, which was large, but open to the weather and not very conveniently situated, was employed largely, though not exclusively, by Shakespeare's company until it was demolished in 1598.

(ii) The 'Curtain,' a smaller structure of the same type as the 'Theatre' was built in 1577 and was still standing in 1627. It was very near the 'Theatre' and originally its rival, but at times was under the same management. It was certainly used by Shakespeare's company in 1598, and the poet Marston alludes to the performance of *Romeo and Juliet* there.

(3) Playhouses south of the Thames, in Surrey.

(i) Newington Butts, an inconveniently situated theatre more than a mile from the river, in use occasionally from 1580 or earlier. In June,

---

1 The Lord Chamberlain wrote to the Lord Mayor of London, Oct. 8, 1594: 'Where my now company of players have been accustomed for the better exercise of their quality, and for the service of her Majesty if need so require, to play this winter time within the city at the Cross Keys in Gracious Street, these are to require and pray your Lordship (the time being such as, thanks to God, there is now no danger of the sickness) to permit and suffer them so to do.'

1594, a combination of the Admiral's and Chamberlain's companies, in which Shakespeare was presumably included, performed there. Among the plays then acted were *Andronicus, The Taming of a Shrew,* and *Hamlet.*[1]

(ii) The 'Rose.' On the Bankside near the southern shore of the Thames, opposite London. Built by Philip Henslowe in 1587. The 'Rose' was circular in shape and more elegant, as well as much more accessible than the 'Theatre.' In 1592 it was used by Lord Strange's company (with which Shakespeare may have been associated), but later was ordinarily tenanted by Shakespeare's chief rivals, the Admiral's men, till 1600, when the latter opened a new theatre, the 'Fortune,' north of London Wall on the opposite side of Finsbury Fields from the 'Theatre' and 'Curtain.' This last theatre, being permanently in the possession of his competitors, was probably never used for Shakespeare's plays.

(iii) The 'Globe,' constructed in 1599, partly of timber taken from the dismantled 'Theatre,' stood near the 'Rose,' which it far surpassed in size and magnificence. It was the usual place for the performance of Shakespeare's plays from the middle of 1599 till it was burned in 1613 in the course of the presentation of *Henry VIII.*[2] A large part of the poet's wealth came from his interest in the 'Globe.'[3]

[Two other playhouses on the Bankside—the

---

1 Probably the pre-Shakespearean version, by Kyd.
2 See ante, p. 114. The 'Globe' was rebuilt in 1614.
3 See ante, pp. 31-32.

'Swan,' built in 1595, and the 'Hope,' built in
1613—do not appear to have been used by
Shakespeare's company.]

(b) Private Theatres.

(1) The Second Blackfriars Playhouse.[1] This
was an indoor theatre as distinguished from the
partially roofless public playhouses. It was constructed by the Burbages in 1596 by throwing
together rooms in the Blackfriars building, near
Temple Bar in an aristocratic residence district
on the northern (London) bank of the Thames.
On account of objections from influential dwellers
in the neighborhood, Shakespeare's company was
not able to act in the Blackfriars till 1609,[2] after
which year it was used as a winter house for the
Globe company. The Blackfriars was termed a
'private' theatre largely as a subterfuge to obviate
the hostility against a public playhouse in the
district. It was private only in the sense that it
catered to the fashionable public, charging high
admission fees and introducing special innova-
tions such as artificial lighting, elaborate music,
and the privilege of sitting on the stage. It came
ultimately to be thought of as a more important
playhouse than the democratic 'Globe,' but not
probably during Shakespeare's lifetime.

(2) Private Theatres for Occasional Performances.

(i) The Royal Palaces. During Shakespeare's
lifetime royalty did not attend playhouses, but

1 There had been a first Blackfriars Theatre, in a different part of
the old monastery, in 1576-1584, but with this Shakespeare was not
concerned.
2 During part of the previous period the Children of the Queen's
Chapel were permitted to act there as tenants of the Burbages.

special performances at court were frequent under Elizabeth and much more numerous under James I. The stage would usually be erected on such occasions in the great hall of the palaces of Greenwich, Whitehall, and Hampton Court. At the Christmas season of 1594, for example, Shakespeare is known to have acted in two comedies before Queen Elizabeth at Greenwich.[1] At Christmas, 1597, *Love's Labour's Lost* was acted before the Queen at Whitehall; and at Christmas, 1603, Shakespeare's company presented a total of six plays before the court of James I at Hampton Court.

(ii) The Inns of Court. Gala performances in the halls of the London Inns of Court, under the auspices of the lawyers who composed the particular 'inn,' were notable events. We have record of the performance of *The Comedy of Errors* at Gray's Inn in 1594[2] and of *Twelfth Night* at the Middle Temple in 1602.[3]

(iii) The Private Houses of Noblemen. In 1605 a performance of *Love's Labour's Lost*, for the amusement of James I's queen, Anne of Denmark, was arranged, to take place either at Lord Southampton's London house or at that of Sir Robert Cecil, Viscount Cranborne.[4] In December, 1603, Shakespeare's company traveled much farther afield and performed before James I at Wilton, the country house of the Earl of Pembroke.

1 See ante, p. 14.
2 See ante, p. 101.
3 See ante, p. 108.
4 See ante, p. 102.

B. Provincial Theatres. Outside of the London district regular theatres did not exist in Shakespeare's time, but performances of his plays were given by his own company throughout the length and breadth of England. Various conditions made it necessary that a London company should spend a considerable part of its time in 'traveling.' These were the hostile attitude of the Mayor and corporation, which sometimes made it impossible to secure an acting place near the city; the discomfort and inaccessibility of the public playhouses in bad weather; periods of financial stringency, when the popularity of some rival attraction temporarily prevented a company from making expenses in London; and, most of all, the constant recurrence of the plague.

The danger of spreading plague infection was continually argued by the opponents of drama in London, and there seems to have been worked out a sort of compromise principle that plays must cease when the reported plague deaths reached the number of thirty or forty a week. 1593, 1603, and 1609 were great plague years, in which there was very little acting in London, and consequently much traveling; but even after Shakespeare's company attained its high and assured position under the special favor of James I, there were few years in which it did not travel for a period. Allusions to this laborious and distasteful mode of life are found in the poet's sonnets,[1] and the first edition of *Hamlet* specifies that the play had been acted in Cambridge and Oxford as well as London. It would seem that traveling professional companies were not permitted to use the college halls of the universities, which were the scene of the local academic plays;

[1] E.g. Sonnets 27, 28, 50, 51.

but in all towns recognized noblemen's companies were entitled to the use of the town halls for their plays. James I's patent to Shakespeare and his fellows definitely grants them the right to act 'within any townhalls, or motehalls, or other convenient places . . . within our said realms and dominions.'[1] The country houses of gentlemen were frequently visited by traveling companies.[2]

---

1 See ante, p. 46.

2 For details of the various provincial towns known to have been visited by Shakespeare's company see J. T. Murray, *English Dramatic Companies*, i. 107-9, 183-4, and E. K. Chambers, *Elizabethan Stage*, ii. 192-220.

THE PERSONALITY OF SHAKESPEARE

The bard of Avon, most successful perhaps of all the poets of the world, owed much of his success to his care in rendering unto Cæsar the things that are Cæsar's, while laying up his finest treasures for generations yet unborn. From his own age Shakespeare asked and obtained 'a fellowship in a cry of players,' with the solid emoluments thereto appertaining. He obtained his ease at the Boar's Head, Mermaid, and the gentle hostelries along the Stratford road. He acquired the arms and title of a gentleman, and ultimately broad meadow lands in Warwickshire, with the spacious leisure of New Place. Willingly he relinquished the regal immortality of Westminster, by the side of Chaucer, Spenser, and Ben Jonson, for undisturbed repose in the chancel of his provincial church.

Once in early life Shakespeare vouchsafed a scant dozen lines[1] of compliment to the Virgin Queen; twice, likewise at the opening of his career, he deigned to dedicate a poem to a noble patron. This is almost the whole extent of Shakespeare's literary concession to his age.[2] The characters of his plays he selected, with what almost seems to us a curious perversity, from Veronese and Frenchmen, Romans, Greeks, Jews, Danes, Moors, and ancient Britons—from every type of people but the subjects of his queen. Of the English of the past he is an unrivaled delineator; of the Englishmen of his own time he hardly tells us directly

---

1 *Midsummer Night's Dream*, II. i. 155-164.

2 The Sonnets contain, perhaps, a further tribute to Southampton. In *Henry V* (Act V, Chorus) he flatters Essex; in *Macbeth* he lauds the progeny of Banquo and offers a testimonial (IV. iii.) to James I's quackery regarding the 'King's evil'; in *The Merry Wives of Windsor* he may consciously have written himself down to the Queen's taste.

anything except that they dress outrageously, outdrink the Dutch, and are stupidly given to staring at strange monsters.[1]

I

The greatest of the Elizabethan romanticists is, in fact, neither so conspicuously Elizabethan nor so transparently romantic as most of his contemporaries. Shakespeare's difference from his fellows is apparent, indeed, in the difficulty we encounter when we seek adjectives to qualify his work. For Spenser and Marlowe, Sidney and Ralegh, it is not so hard to find expressive and satisfying characterizations: the critic of Shakespeare is thrown back upon paradox. The greatest English writer is in many ways one of the least literary; the most brilliant constructor of plot one of the least inventive; the most successful searcher of the human heart one of the least obviously subtle. Shakespeare was neither an artist in the sense in which Spenser was, nor a romanticist as Ralegh was, nor an intellectualist as Marlowe was. Wisdom is perhaps the only attribute which we can apply to him without need of qualification.

And Shakespeare's wisdom was not of the kind which colleges supply. We need no biographical evidence to assure us that the author of the plays was not indebted to the universities; and the academic attitude on the part of his critics has often proved the least profitable of all. Ben Jonson and Samuel Johnson and Dryden, for example, have said splendidly true things of Shakespeare when they spoke, unofficially as it were, from the depth of their robust humanity; and each has

---

[1] *Merchant of Venice*, I. ii. 70 ff.; *Othello*, II. iii. 79 ff.; *Tempest*, II. ii. 29 ff.

been signally unfortunate when essaying to write of him from the chair of a literary dictator. The clearest light on this poet has often emanated, not from academic halls, but from the experience of those who have rather taken degrees in what old Gower calls the University of all the world—in Shakespeare's university.

A chief reason why formal criticism has proved so barren is simply that Shakespeare—more even than most other romantic writers—attained his art by indirection. A straight line, indeed, is seldom the shortest line between a romantic poet's inspiration and his accomplishment; but in Shakespeare the usual Elizabethan carelessness about rules of poetry may often seem magnified into carelessness about poetry itself. 'The works of Shakespeare,' says Coleridge, 'are romantic poetry revealing itself in the drama.' But his romanticism requires to be distinguished from that of his great contemporaries. In the sense that the romanticist is one who ignores academic rules for writing, Shakespeare is a very type and pattern of the romantic dramatist; but he has nothing of that other, more advanced, romanticism which marks Spenser and Marlowe as conscious innovators and revolutionists, battling for ideas which they know to be strange and love therefor. He has nothing of the romanticism which produced *Hernani*. Shakespeare's romanticism did not lead him to affect originality or to despise precedent; nor did it impel him to establish new rules for dramatic writing. Mr. Munro hardly exaggerates when he says in the preface to the *Shakespeare Allusion Book:* 'Shakespeare, like all the great poets of the world, left no school behind him. He was not an initiator; he invented no new style; he introduced no new vogue.'

Shakespeare was constitutionally incapable of doing what Lyly, Marlowe, and Ben Jonson successively did—of inventing a perfectly characteristic new type of drama, and then consistently illustrating it in his practice. Probably he would have been incapable of offering concerning the dramatist's art any views as definite as Hamlet expresses about the actor's. What he created in the way of dramatic style and structure— and it was, of course, a great deal—seems to have come to him as the result of practice rather than specu- lation. What he borrowed—and it was even more— found its way into his plays by chance more often than by critical choice. In the controversy between classic and romantic theories of drama—between Jonson's method and Marlowe's—Shakespeare seems to take no stand and feel no interest. It happens that two par- ticularly romantic plays, *The Tempest* and *Othello*, are in their structure nearly as classic (regular) as two of Jonson's, while two plays of classic atmosphere and story, *Julius Cæsar* and *Antony and Cleopatra*, carry to the farthest extreme the romantic irregu- larities. For these things—for the whole formal side of poetry—Shakespeare doubtless cared as little as Homer. Like Homer, he can hardly be designated as either romantic or classic; and more than any other modern he has succeeded in making his art seem coex- tensive with life, in arrogating to himself Pope's fine claim for Homer:

'To follow nature is to follow him.'

It is the indirectness of Shakespeare's art that here accounts for its wonderful success. The perfectly clear light in which his men and women are seen implies a perfect lack of self-consciousness in their portrayer, and with this we can very safely credit him. Shakespeare was in no way a literary critic. His taste in books does not seem to have been good, if we may judge by some of the poor works he chooses to dramatize and by the many great ones he ignores. Compared with his most worthy contemporaries, Shakespeare rather lacked the literary conscience. Compared, that is, with Lyly, Marlowe, or Jonson, he was not more, but less careful in choosing and developing his plot, in shaping his sentences, and in winding up his conclusions.

II

Had Shakespeare been the sort of man that he is thought to have been by those who identify him with Francis or with Anthony Bacon, or with Ralegh, or with Marlowe, or with Rutland or Southampton, or with Edward de Vere, Earl of Oxford, or with William Stanley, Earl of Derby—that is, had he been well-bred and college-trained, all this, we may feel sure, would have been different. He would have been more precocious and more clever. In all human probability he would have been much less wise. He would have been more fastidious about accuracy of detail in sentence structure, in plot construction, and in plausibility of incident and local color. He would have sought the appearance of originality more and attained the substance less.

One great strength of Shakespeare's dramatic art lies in the fact that circumstances made him a great connoisseur of life and a very careless student of literature. He was first an actor, second a practical adapter of old plays, third a company manager. Only fourth and last was he a dramatist proper. No other Eliza-

bethan writer[1] had so many and such intimate points
of contact with the whole business of the theatre. A
very important reason for Shakespeare's superiority
to his contemporaries is that he was not primarily a
gentleman author like Lyly, Greene, Peele, Marlowe,
but actually, as Greene called him, 'an absolute Johannes factotum' of the theatre, a man too absorbed in
opening the world's oyster—in holding the mirror up
to life—to feel much the littlenesses and compunctions
of the artist.

From these general, and rather trite, remarks two
truths can be deduced. One is that Shakespeare is not,
as he seems often to be thought, the summation of
Elizabethan literary art. The student of Shakespeare
will know much of human nature, but not a vast deal
about the sixteenth-century mind. Shakespeare was
indeed *not* of one age, and did not supersede Lyly and
Spenser and Marlowe and Jonson as exponents of his
era.

The other truth is that the problems of Shakespeare's great plays are not to be settled triumphantly
by frontal literary attack, by disquisitions upon his
mind and art alone. The personality of Shakespeare
has been so dismally disputed that students have sometimes been driven to wish the whole matter buried in
Cimmerian gloom. Thus Dr. Furness[2] attempts to
lighten ship by merrily bidding the man Shakespeare
begone with all his mystery:

'It is merely our ignorance which creates the mystery. To Shakespeare's friends and daily companions
there was nothing mysterious in his life; on the con-
trary, it possibly appeared to them as unusually dull
and commonplace. It certainly had no incidents so far

1 Thomas Heywood is his nearest competitor.
2 Preface to *Much Ado about Nothing*, Variorum edition.

out of the common that they thought it worth while to record them. Shakespeare never killed a man as Jonson did; his voice was never heard, like Marlowe's, in tavern brawls; nor was he ever, like Marston and Chapman, threatened with the penalty of having his ears lopped and his nose split; but his life was so gentle and so clear in the sight of man and of Heaven that no record of it has come down to us; for which failure I am fervently grateful, and as fervently hope that no future year will ever reveal even the faintest peep through the divinity which doth hedge this king.'

Unfortunately, it is precisely the man Shakespeare —in some circles derisively called the Stratfordian— who carries with him into obscurity the dramatic artist. Without him—ill-bred, ill-lettered, and in some ways perhaps ill-balanced as he was—the plays lose their coherent meaning and disintegrate into picture puzzles, in which mad ladies and gentlemen piece out the names and features of whom they will.

There was once a time when it seemed a mark of daring and original thought to assert the identity of Francis Bacon with the author of the Shakespearean dramas. That time is now past, and the mere Baconian is in sorry plight. His doctrine is as hackneyed as that of the Shakespearean, and it lacks the compensating satisfaction of reason. There are few joys in being illogical, when one must also be flat. Desperate cases produce desperate remedies, and super-Baconians have lately arisen, ready to supplant the pale ineffectual fires of their predecessors by yet brighter blazes of assumption. Such is the late E. G. Harman (*Edmund Spenser and the Impersonations of Francis Bacon,* 1914), who devotes 592 pages to proving that Bacon wrote not merely Shakespeare, but also all of Spenser.

Such is Mr. Parker Woodward, who in 1912 included among *Francis Bacon's Works* (*Acknowledged, Vizarded, or Suspected*) those of Lyly, Greene, Spenser, Shakespeare, Kyd, Peele, Marlowe, Gosson, Bright, Burton, Webbe, Nashe, Watson, and others, including a part of Ben Jonson's. And such is Peter Alvor, who in 1911 (*Anthony Bacon: Die Lösung des Shakespeare-Problems*) pointed out that the Bacon who wrote Shakespeare was not Francis, but his brother Anthony.

Of late years, however, the preachers of Shakespearean dissent have manifested a tendency to abandon Bacon in order to exploit newer aspirants to the laurel. The revelation of Mr. J. C. Nicol, in *The Real Shakespeare,* is couched in mystical language: 'I, Fortinbras, otherwise Posthumus, quarried and on 7th December, 1905, plainly discovered Henry Wriotheslie, third Earl of Southampton, undoubtedly to be the sole Author and begetter of the so-called poems and plays known as Shakespeare's Works . . . producing innumerable offspring in Art, with other various names, notably (as Marlowe) from the age of 13.' A contemporary work by Peter Alvor (*Das neue Shakespeare-Evangelium,* ca. 1907) ascribed Shakespeare to a judicious partnership between the Earls of Southampton and Rutland. In 1912 M. Célestin Demblon (Socialist Deputy from Liège) maintained through 559 pages the thesis: *Lord Rutland est Shakespeare*. In 1914, the late Henry Pemberton, Jr., did as much for Ralegh in *Shakespeare and Sir Walter Ralegh*. In 1919 appeared the two impressive volumes of Professor Abel Lefranc, in nomination of another candidate: *Sous le Masque de "William Shakespeare": William Stanley VIᵉ Comte de Derby;* and in 1920 the most portentous perhaps of all these colossal works, Mr. J. Thomas Looney's *"Shakespeare" Identified in Edward de Vere, the Seventeenth Earl of Oxford.*

III

The desire to see the face behind the mask is not only legitimate, but necessary; and, happily, it has not recently been exclusively confined to the Bacon-Ralegh-Oxford-Derby-Rutland-Southampton exponents of critical solitaire. The most priceless hour of the irrecoverable past, says William Archer,[1] would be that in which one might meet the real Shakespeare face to face; and Professor Bradley says: 'For my own part I confess that, though I should care nothing about the man if he had not written the works, yet, since we possess them, I would rather see and hear him for five minutes in his proper person than discover a new one.'

The author of the Shakespearean plays, we can say with perfect confidence, was not the advanced political thinker that Bacon was, or Ralegh, or Spenser, or even Marlowe. He was distinctly a traditionalist in politics and social theory. His attitude toward the state and sovereign was not Tudor, but Plantagenet; not renaissance, but feudal. It represents the feeling of Stratford much better than that of London.

The King in Shakespeare is nearly always the man

---

1 'If some enchanter should offer to recover for me a single hour of the irrecoverable past, I think I should choose to be placed among the audience at the Globe Theatre, in or about the year 1600, with liberty to run round between the acts and interview the author-actor-manager, Master Shakespeare, in his tiring room. For this I would give—one can afford to be lavish in bidding for the inconceivable—say a year of my life. There is nothing more difficult than to form a vivid and satisfactory picture of the material conditions under which Shakespeare worked; and there is nothing more fascinating than the attempt to do so.'

on horseback. He who rides roan Barbary[1] gets the plaudits of the multitude; and Shakespeare's voice can generally be heard among the rest, crying with quite old-fashioned vehemence: 'Le Roi est mort; Vive le Roi!' Shakespeare's kings, it has been said, are always kingly; and so they are in the old Plantagenet sense. They go to bed with their crowns on, and sleep with the sceptre under their pillow. They brandish swords and throw down warders, and make polished speeches, which, in a surprising number of the examples, lack moral or psychological sincerity.

Shakespeare's loyalty was always that of the Tory country-dweller. No length of years in London, no number of performances at court, sufficed to obliterate the country boy's impression of the vague exotic splendor of the crown. His is not the personal devotion of the cavalier to Charles, nor the imperial ardor of such typical Elizabethans as Spenser and Ralegh. It is rather the old feudal attitude of the Wars of the Roses, the attitude of the Yorkist who would have fought for the crown of England though he found it on a thistle bush. There is every reason for believing that Shakespeare was quite satisfied with the *de facto* principle of sovereignty which Prince Hal expounds to his father:

> 'My gracious liege,
> You won it, wore it, kept it, gave it me.
> Then plain and right must my possession be.'[2]

Perhaps it is not altogether an accident that in Shakespeare's biography the careless continuators of the old feudal England—Southampton and Essex and Pembroke—mean a great deal, and the purveyors of

---

1 *Richard II*, V. v 76-94.
2 *2 Henry IV*, IV. v. 219 ff.

the new political faith—Burghley, Ralegh, and Walsingham—mean nothing.

Shakespeare's patriotism also, glowing though it is, is traditional and essentially pre-Elizabethan. He has nothing of the new imperialism so dominant in Ralegh and Spenser, and very little indeed of the sense of the gorgeous Indies and the new world beyond the seas that Marlowe shows everywhere. He was distinctly a 'little Englander.' He glories in the thought of the aloofness and self-sufficiency of his island,

> 'This scepter'd isle,
> This earth of majesty, this seat of Mars,
> This other Eden, demi-Paradise,
> This fortress built by Nature for herself.'[1]

His vision stops at the ideal of a hermit kingdom, free from foreign entanglements, safe in the unity of its citizens and in a proudly defensive attitude toward the world:

> 'This England never did, nor never shall
> Lie at the proud foot of a conqueror,
> But when it first did help to wound itself.
> Now these her princes are come home again,
> Come the three corners of the world in arms,
> And we shall shock them.'[2]

Wars abroad are for him but sallies from the fortress, heroic, yet of dubious advisability. Henry the Fifth has prudential and legalistic aims in invading France, but no imperial aims. He embarks upon his expedition because his crafty father has advised him to end civil discord in England by busying 'giddy minds with

---

1 *Richard II*, II. i. 40 ff.
2 *King John*, V. vii. 112 ff.

foreign quarrels';[1] and because the Archbishop of Canterbury has unblushingly ventured an affirmative answer to his question, 'May I with right and conscience make this claim?'[2] Shakespeare shirks the real business of the conquest of France, and concentrates attention upon the upset of all sporting predictions in the outcome of the battle of Agincourt. And Agincourt is particularly glorified as a defensive action. Says Henry to the French herald, Montjoy,

> 'Turn thee back,
> And tell thy king I do not seek him now,
> But could be willing to march on to Calais
> Without impeachment.'[3]

If only the French would not insist upon it, there should be no conquest of France. The Jingoes, pray observe, are all in the French camp—all but Captain Macmorris, the Irishman, who by Gower's account (and his own) is 'a very valiant gentleman' and a fire-eater, and for whom we have Fluellen's unimpeachable authority that 'he is an ass, as in the world: I will verify as much in his peard: he has no more directions in the two disciplines of the wars, look you . . . than is a puppy-dog.'[4]

Shakespeare learned his patriotism and foreign policy from Holinshed and the other old chroniclers who followed in the train of that prince of sporting-writers, Froissart. They treated warfare as we treat football—as a spectacular, exciting, and fundamentally good-natured pastime, arising from no particular causes except the love of competition and productive of no consequences except the glory of the successful

1 *2 Henry IV*, IV. v. 212.
2 *Henry V*, I. ii. 96.
3 Ibid. III. vi. 151 ff.
4 Ibid. III. ii. 78 ff.

athlete.   King Henry's speech before Agincourt is
the high-water mark of football oratory:

> 'This day is called the feast of Crispian:
> He that outlives this day, and comes safe home,
> Will stand a-tiptoe when this day is nam'd,
> And rouse him at the name of Crispian.
> He that shall live this day and see old age,
> Will yearly on the vigil feast his neighbours,
> And say, "To-morrow is Saint Crispian":
> Then will he strip his sleeve and show his scars,
> And say, "These wounds I had on Crispin's day."
> Old men forget: yet all shall be forgot,
> But he'll remember with advantages
> What feats he did that day. Then shall our names,
> Familiar in his mouth as household words,
> Harry the king, Bedford and Exeter,
> Warwick and Talbot, Salisbury and Gloucester,
> Be in their flowing cups freshly remember'd.
> This story shall the good man teach his son;
> And Crispin Crispian shall ne'er go by,
> From this day to the ending of the world,
> But we in it shall be remembered.'

This was not the spirit in which Queen Elizabeth
made war.   It was not the spirit of the seven thousand English whom the Earl of Essex led to Rouen in
1591 to aid Navarre's stern Huguenots against the
Catholic League.   There is more zeal for national ex-
pansion and contemporary foreign policy in the one
play of *Edward III* (I think, by Peele) than in all
that Shakespeare wrote.

The very sea, which to Ralegh and Spenser was ever
beckoning Englishmen abroad, which was Cynthia's
peculiar domain and highway, is to Shakespeare a de-

fensive wall, a moat, whose purpose was to shut off
alien lands from

> 'this little world,
> This precious stone set in the silver sea,
> Which serves it in the office of a wall,
> Or as a moat defensive to a house.'[1]

The England he apostrophizes is not the mistress of
the ocean, but

> 'England bound in with the triumphant sea,
> Whose rocky shore beats back the envious siege
> Of watery Neptune.'[1]

What must one of Drake's sea-dogs, whose home was
on the billows, have thought if he blundered into a
performance of *Richard II* and heard John of Gaunt
discoursing in so land-lubberish a fashion? There is
nothing that would justify us in assuming that Shakespeare's heart e'er within him burned with desire to
board a sea-going vessel, or that he ever cared to join
the Elizabethan crowds which flocked down to Dept-
ford to visit Drake's *Golden Hind*. There is nothing
to show that he caught the oceanic swell and surge
which so resounds in the famous note that Drake and
his colleagues sent ashore after the first days of the
Armada fight (Aug. 1, 1588):

'We whose names are hereunder written have determined and agreed in council to follow and pursue the
Spanish fleet until we have cleared our own coast and
brought the Frith[2] west of us, and then to return back
again, as well to revictual our ships (which stand in
extreme scarcity) as also to guard and defend our own
coast at home. With further protestation that if our

1 *Richard II*, II. i. 45 ff., 61 ff.
2 Firth of Forth.

wants of victuals and munitions were supplied we would pursue them to the furthest that they durst have gone.'

After reading the history plays it is with wonder and astonishment that one follows a certain present-day tendency to explain Shakespeare as a literary Talleyrand or Machiavelli, writing for the purpose of shaping public policy and disseminating political propaganda. Strange it is to see one speculative critic defining the plays of Shakespeare as the unique sourcebook of English history betweeen 1588 and 1603, explaining that when Froude closed his narrative at the year 1588 and Gardiner refrained from commencing before 1603, it can only have been because those mere historians realized that they might not hope, without becoming Shakespeare scholars, to understand what really happened in the intervening fifteen years. Strange also it is, and doubtless mirth-provoking to the souls below, to learn that *Hamlet* was written to explain the murder of Amy Robsart—or, as another tells us, to explain the assassination of Lord Darnley; and to be informed that *Love's Labour's Lost* was written to frustrate the purposes of Lord Burghley, and *A Midsummer Night's Dream* to secure the crown of England for the Earl of Derby—or else for the so-called 'Suffolk heir,' Lord Hertford's son.

One fancies that Shakespeare's soul is surprised at these things, and not a little flattered; for in his mortal days that entrancing, brilliant moss-back, Will Shakespeare, must have been one of the last men in London with whom an up-to-date Elizabethan would have thought of discussing politics, or religion, or geography, or current affairs. Prince Bismarck is said to have characterized his compatriots as political

dunces: one foresees a day when the German apprecia-
tors of Shakespeare (to whom we continue to owe so
much) will on this ground also set up a claim to intellectual affinity with our poet.

The prejudices of the country-bred youth persist
also in Shakespeare's treatment of the various classes
of English society. He has the old-fashioned rustic's
fondness for lords and ladies and for country squires,
and for all the functionaries that go in their train:
footmen and porters, hostlers, tapsters, gardeners,
and pedlars.[1] The plain tiller of the soil gets loving
treatment, from Costard in *Love's Labour's Lost* to the
charming Egyptian Clown in *Antony and Cleopatra;*
and he offers conspicuous homage to the Cotswold
shepherds in *As You Like It* and in *The Winter's Tale.*

The denizens of the city, on the other hand,—with
honorable exception of the tavern drawers,—seldom
evoke Shakespeare's interest. The Lord Mayor and
Aldermen, the livery companies, law clerks, and ap-
prentices, the Puritan sectaries, and cut-purses, and
street-singers—all the picturesque and bizarrely dif-
ferentiated types that made up the pride, pomp, and
circumstance, as well as the bustle and romantic un-
certainties, of Elizabethan London—whom Dekker
painted so lovingly and Jonson with such microscopic
fidelity—are by Shakespeare referred to little and dis-
praisingly. The 'velvet-guards and Sunday citizens'[2]
and the whole shop-keeping class, from the apothecary
in *Romeo and Juliet* down, arouse at best his pity and
almost invariably his scorn. They are used most to
barb the point of his contemptuous metaphors. The
rude mechanicals, or city artisans, are dull and pom-
pous, and the great body of citizens is the *mobile vulgus*

1 Note the groom in *Richard II.*
2 *1 Henry IV,* III. i. 260.

and nothing more, an object equally of derision and distrust.

A single striking example may illustrate the point. There was one rough, roystering, and unique set of Londoners who must have come under constant observation of a man doing business on the Bankside. It was the tribe of watermen or scullers, a body numbering its hundreds, if not thousands, and possessed even of its laureate in Taylor the Water-Poet. Indisputably, Shakespeare must have sat *tête à tête* with dozens of them on the way to Southwark, and his fortune can hardly have been so bad that he met only the dull dogs in so hilarious a fraternity. Yet he never came nearer to a tribute than when in *Othello* he let drop his casual slur on

'A knave of common hire, a gondolier.'

Are we not almost justified in thinking that the well-styled Bard of *Avon* (not Thames) was the converse of Peter Bell? A primrose by the water's brim was to Shakespeare all that it was to Wordsworth, but the delectable Taylor was to him, I sadly fear, simply 'a knave of common hire,' and he was nothing more. We may find in this a reason why Shakespeare never chose to write a city comedy. Here again, then, there is in Shakespeare more of Stratford than of London, more of Plantagenet than of Tudor England.

In religion also Shakespeare evidently did not feel the attraction of the new ideas which so appealed to Spenser, Marlowe, and Ralegh. There is no good reason for believing that he was an actual recusant, a convinced disciple of the Roman faith; but the religious penumbra of his mind was certainly archaic. For poetic purposes at least religion still connoted for him friars, masses, vigils, extreme unction, and purgatory. It came natural to him to invoke angels and ministers of grace, to swear by Our Lady and Saint Patrick.

Nor can we doubt, rare as are the authentic expressions of Shakespeare's personal feeling in his works, that the poet was himself fully aware of the homely and conservative cast of all his thinking. Readers have always, and rightly, recognized the inner voice of the dramatist's own conviction in the words with which Biron abjures

> 'Taffeta phrases, silken term precise,
> Three-pil'd hyperboles, spruce affectation,
> Figures pedantical.'

'I do forswear them,' says Biron, 'and I here protest . . .
Henceforth my wooing mind shall be express'd
In russet yeas and honest kersey noes.'[1]

The volatile Biron, it is probable, found the vow too hard to keep; but for Shakespeare, who here speaks through him, russet and kersey were to the end the only wear. In his seventy-sixth Sonnet he expresses, with a candid clarity impossible to discount, his realization of the intellectual gulf which separated him from the peacock race of the true Elizabethans:

'Why is my verse so barren of new pride,
So far from variation or quick change?
Why with the time do I not glance aside
To new-found methods and to compounds strange?
Why write I still all one, ever the same,
And keep invention in a noted weed,
That every word doth almost tell my name,
Showing their birth, and where they did proceed?'

1 *Love's Labour's Lost*, V. ii. 407 ff.

IV

The reader, therefore, who knows only Shakespeare among the Elizabethans, will get relatively very little of the intellectual atmosphere in which Milton and other Londoners of the next generation grew up. He will get less of this from Shakespeare than from any other eminent writer of the period.

The greatest of modern poets passed a quarter century amid the tremendous intellectual currents—social, religious, and imperial—of Elizabethan London, and his soul through all this time remained a stranger to them. 'Multum incola fuit anima sua.' His most apparent efforts to reflect the spirit around him are the relative failures of *Love's Labour's Lost* and *The Merry Wives of Windsor.* He gave his audiences, to be sure, what they liked immensely, but he gave it with a strange and stubborn indirectness. The Armada comes and goes; Drake and Ralegh light the beacons of a new and potent patriotism; and Shakespeare tunes his native woodland harp to sing, in *Henry V,* the praises of an obsolete Lancastrian policy. Great Britain has its birth in the union of Scotland and England, and Shakespeare weaves into *Macbeth* a musty dynastic compliment to the new monarch.

The London bookstalls groan with pamphlets about the discovery of Bermuda and the colonization of Virginia, about cannibals and noble savages, and the Isle of Devils and the Fountain of Perpetual Youth. Drayton, Shakespeare's contemporary, friend, and neighbor in Warwickshire, writes his ecstatic stanzas, *To the Virginian Voyage,* urging all

> 'brave heroic minds,
> Worthy your country's name,

> (Whilst loitering hinds
> Lurk here at home with shame)'

to

> 'Go and subdue . . .
> Virginia, Earth's only paradise.'

In the play of *Eastward Ho* (1605) even the gravity of Chapman, the local realism of Jonson and Marston, succumb to the infection; and in the speeches of Captain Seagull this comedy of London manners grows iridescent with fanciful hyperboles of Virginian opportunity.

'I tell thee,' says Captain Seagull, as he basks in the admiration of his tavern companions, 'gold is more plentiful there than copper is with us; and for as much red copper as I can bring, I'll have thrice the weight in gold. Why, man, all their dripping pans . . . are pure gold; and all the chains with which they chain up their streets are massy gold; all the prisoners they take are fettered in gold; and for rubies and diamonds, they go forth on holidays and gather 'em by the seashore, to hang on their children's coats and stick in their caps, as commonly as our children wear saffron-gilt brooches and groats with holes in 'em.

Scapethrift. And is it a pleasant country withal?

Seagull. As ever the sun shined on; temperate and full of all sorts of excellent viands; wild boar is as common there as our tamest bacon is here, venison as mutton. And then you shall live freely there, without serjeants, or courtiers, or lawyers, or intelligencers.'[1]

Such tavern talk has a veritable ring. The Boar's Head in Eastcheap must have echoed with it; and one

---

1 *Eastward Ho*, by Marston, Chapman, and Jonson, III. iii.

wonders what ailed Will Shakespeare that it never found a lodging in his brain. For him El Dorado never ceased to be located somewhere among his native Cotswold hills, and he never conceived a vision of more radiant and infectious felicity than that picture of Master Shallow's orchard, 'where, in an arbour, we will eat a last year's pippin of my own graffing, with a dish of caraways, and so forth;'[1] while Cousin Silence grows amiably drunk, and the good varlet Davy unfolds the merits of an arrant knave, William Visor of Wincot, who must needs be countenanced against the honest man, Clement Perkes of the Hill.

Spenser's vision leaps from East to Western Ind, dilating on 'th' Indian Peru,' 'the Amazon's huge river,' or 'fruitfullest Virginia,' invoking ceaselessly

> 'the beaten mariner,
> That long hath wandred in the ocean wide,
> Oft sous'd in swelling Tethys' saltish tear.'

In Marlowe, Tamburlaine dreams of

> 'East India and the late discover'd isles,'

Barrabas of

> 'The merchants of the Indian mines,
> That trade in metal of the purest mould,'

and Faustus of the 'huge argosies' that drag

> 'from America the golden fleece
> That yearly stuffs old Philip's treasury.'

Shakespeare never mentions Virginia and names America only once, in the early *Comedy of Errors*. Once, in a bit of comic prose, he lets Maria allude with betraying carelessness to 'the new map with the aug-

[1] *2 Henry IV*, V. iii.

mentation of the Indies.'[1]   Contrast the inspirational
potency of maps and globes for Marlowe, Hakluyt,
and Spenser!   Finally Shakespeare offers belated and
grudging acquiescence to the spirit of discovery by
telling (in his last complete play) how a Duke of
Milan and his daughter once went voyaging in the
Mediterranean in

> 'A rotten carcass of a boat; not rigg'd,
> Nor tackle, sail, nor mast,'—[2]

and how they found there an enchanted isle—forsooth,
not far from Tunis and Algiers!

V

Shakespeare did not bring with him from Stratford
a very plastic, or, as we should say, a trained, mind.
He brought limitations and prejudices which he never
outgrew.   He also brought three things that matter
more: an unaccountable genius; a tremendous capacity
for hard work; and an extraordinary interest in men
and women, based on a various, and not impeccable, experience of them.

He did not bring with him, as Horatio did (or said
he did), a truant disposition, but one already fixed in
the course it must pursue.   Undoubtedly the emotional-
ist and the thinker had at one time struggled within
him: Richard the Second with Bolingbroke, Romeo
with Mercutio, Hotspur with Falstaff.   Undoubtedly
the time had been when emotion had held sway, and
Shakespeare was both a sadder and wiser man thereby.
But that time, we may be sure, was over before ever
Shakespeare saw London and commenced dramatist.
In all that he wrote for the stage, in the sonnets too,

[1] *Twelfth Night*, III. ii. 88.
[2] *Tempest*, I. ii. 146.

and even in the poems, which Hazlitt likens to 'a couple of ice-houses . . . as hard, as glittering, and as cold,' thought and reflection transcend emotion. From Biron in *Love's Labour's Lost* to Prospero in *The Tempest*, Shakespeare elaborates the principle that thought is the very core of life and feeling but its outer husk. 'There is nothing either good or bad but thinking makes it so.'[1] His two greatest figures, the two who are most truly representative of him, Hamlet and Falstaff, are men of thought, not men of feeling, and not men of action. So in their different ways are Ulysses and Brutus, Henry the Fifth and Iago. In Cleopatra he paints not the witchery that inflames the passions, but that which unhinges the intellect. It is the Serpent, not the Siren, that he sees, and Antony sums her up in the words:

> 'She is *cunning* past man's *thought*.'[2]

Where Marlowe pictures human aspiration as resulting from the clash of unresting and irreconcilable emotions, and declares:

> 'Nature that framed us of four elements,
> Still warring in our breasts for regiment . . .
> Wills us to wear ourselves and never rest,'

Shakespeare views human character as the quiet consequence of the 'godlike reason' of the thinking animal:

> 'Sure, he that made us with such large discourse,
> Looking before and after, gave us not
> That capability and godlike reason
> To fust in us unus'd.'[3]

It is again the thinking side of man that Hamlet

[1] *Hamlet*, II. ii. 259.
[2] *Antony and Cleopatra*, I. ii. 155.
[3] *Hamlet*, IV. iv. 36 ff.

stresses in the words which better than any others explain what attracted Shakespeare to the study of human psychology:

'What a piece of work is a man! How noble in reason! how infinite in faculty . . . in apprehension how like a god.'[1]

Shakespeare was as comparatively little interested in concrete incident as he was in abstract emotion. The overt act generally has no special significance for him. He was no pragmatist, as Bacon was, and would never have agreed with Bacon that 'good thoughts (though God accept them) yet towards men are little better than good dreams, except they be put in act.'[2]

The spectrum of life, running from dreams through thoughts into acts, was for the true Elizabethans brightest at the two ends. It was the glory and the weakness alike of Sidney, Spenser, and Ralegh, of Tamburlaine and Faustus, that they saw gorgeous emotional dreams passing directly into brilliant acts. The Scythian Shepherd speaks for them all when he says:

> 'I am strongly mov'd
> That if I should desire the Persian crown,
> I could attain it with a wondrous ease.'

Their imaginations, in truth, were all clad in seven-league boots, and made but one careless step of the whole way from the violet of the earliest vision to the red of final accomplishment. It especially distinguishes Shakespeare that he kept his eye upon the middle of the spectrum, on that vital and revealing 'interim' of which Brutus speaks,

1 *Hamlet*, II. ii. 323 ff.
2 *Of Great Place.*

> 'Between the acting of a dreadful thing
> And the first motion.'[1]

The deeds themselves mattered much less to Shakespeare. It is doubtful whether he would have cared to consider whether Hamlet actually did too little or Othello too much. Play after play shows in the carelessness of its closing scenes how rapidly his interest cooled when all the good thinking was over and it remained to reveal the tangible consequences of thought.

So in Shakespeare's actual life he ignored the dreams of El Dorado and imperial England, and he ignored the facts of tobacco and the colonization of Virginia and the Fight of the Revenge, while scrutinizing day by day the thinking minds of the men and women about him. And thereby he gained a wisdom so deep that it concealed his plentiful lack of knowledge—a humanity so immense that we seldom note how completely he had failed to be Elizabethan.

[1] *Julius Cæsar*, II. i. 63.

GENERAL INDEX

(For detailed list of biographical documents relating to
Shakespeare see Table of Contents)

Addenbrooke, John: sued by Shakespeare, 57-59.

Admiral, the Lord (Earl of Nottingham): his company of
players, 131.

Alleyn, Edward, actor: spurious letter to him, mentioning
Shakespeare, 99.

All's Well that Ends Well (originally known as *Love's Labour's Won?*): date, 121; metrical features, 127.

Antony and Cleopatra: entry on Stationers' Register, 116;
small use of prose, 124; metrical features, 127; structure,
139.

Arden, Mary (Shakespeare's mother): 1, 2, 7-9, 16, 38; her
burial, 57.

Arden, Robert (Shakespeare's grandfather): 1, 2, 7, 16, 33.

Arden, Thomas: 2.

Armin, Robert: one of 'King's Men,' 46, 49; mentioned in A.
Phillips' will, 52; principal actor in Shakespeare's plays,
96.

As You Like It: entry on Stationers' Register, 116; metrical
features, 127; alluded to, 151.

Asbies (property of Shakespeare's mother): 7-9.

Bacon, Anne: tenant of Blackfriars property, 71; deceased
mother of M. Bacon, Jr., 79; wife of Mathias Bacon of
Gray's Inn, 81.

Bacon, Francis: 'Baconian' and related theories of authorship, 140, 142-144; quoted, 159.

Bacon, Mathias (Mathie) of Gray's Inn: vendor of Blackfriars property to Henry Walker, 71.

Bacon, Matthew (Mathie): son of the foregoing, 81; sued
in chancery by Shakespeare and others, 78-81.

Bacon, Richard (citizen of London): one of the appellants
in the Blackfriars petition, 79, 80.

Bankside (Surrey): Shakespeare's residence there, 20; theatres on, 131-132.

Barker, Henry: heir of John B., 59-63.